To Zandria...

With love
        and light
and gratitude for
        every day

Love,
Mandy Peckinpah
2014

♡

HOW TO SURVIVE THE WORST THAT CAN HAPPEN

*A Parent's Step by Step Guide to
Healing After the Loss of a Child*

SANDY PECKINPAH

BALBOA.
PRESS
A DIVISION OF HAY HOUSE

Balboa Press books may be ordered through booksellers or by contacting:

Balboa Press
A Division of Hay House
1663 Liberty Drive
Bloomington, IN 47403
www.balboapress.com
1-(877) 407-4847

Because of the dynamic nature of the Internet, any web addresses or links contained in this book may have changed since publication and may no longer be valid. The views expressed in this work are solely those of the author and do not necessarily reflect the views of the publisher, and the publisher hereby disclaims any responsibility for them.

The author of this book does not dispense medical advice or prescribe the use of any technique as a form of treatment for physical, emotional, or medical problems without the advice of a physician, either directly or indirectly. The intent of the author is only to offer information of a general nature to help you in your quest for emotional and spiritual well-being. In the event you use any of the information in this book for yourself, which is your constitutional right, the author and the publisher assume no responsibility for your actions.

Any people depicted in stock imagery provided by Thinkstock are models, and such images are being used for illustrative purposes only. Certain stock imagery © Thinkstock.

Printed in the United States of America.

ISBN: 978-1-4525-8226-9 (sc)
ISBN: 978-1-4525-8228-3 (hc)
ISBN: 978-1-4525-8227-6 (e)

Library of Congress Control Number: 2013916739

Balboa Press rev. date: 02/24/2014

To my beautiful boy, Garrett, who changed my life, forever.

Table of Contents

A FOREWORD FROM
MELISSA GILBERT

First of all…I want to say that if you have the need to purchase this book, I am so very sorry for your loss. The title of the book says it all. You have been through the worst that can happen and know that you have my deepest sympathy and prayers.

I will not tell you that I understand what you're going through. Truthfully, I absolutely cannot. Though I did watch first hand, as my best friend, Sandy, and her family walked through an unthinkable trauma, so I was able to bear witness from when her dear son, Garrett, first passed away right up until now.

I have read this book repeatedly and I can promise you that this is the book you need. There are many others written on the subject of losing a child, but as far as my research has shown, none of them provide you with the step-by-step practicalities you need to get through this unfathomably horrible loss. Most of what Sandy learned, as she and her sweet family walked through it is right here on these pages. But it is not simply a narrative of her story; it's a step-by-step way that you can participate in your own healing, as well as those of your family and loved ones.

It is a simple book to follow with powerful ideas and suggestions that will help. I promise that you will come through this, and at the other end, you will find hope and even relief from your crushing pain. Sandy has laid it out chapter by chapter, perfectly. Follow her steps, make them your own.

This book will help you, not only to walk through your grief day by day, it will provide you with a detailed memory book of your child. It will show you how to journal, not only the loss you experienced and the road to healing, but in it you will find suggestions on how to create memories in your home and how to save your sweet child's milestones as well as things he or she touched and created.

In a way, to me, it can serve not only as a book of hope and healing, it is another baby book for you to chronicle your child's birth into a new life. I do hope you do not find that last sentence to seem harsh or flippant in any way but, what you are experiencing with your child's passing is a transition. I know it is small comfort, after all, you are letting go of the most important thing in your entire life. I just want to express my own feelings that death is, in fact another birth, if you will. A re-birth into the arms of God, Jesus, Buddha, Krishna, Allah, Mohammed... whatever you personally believe in.

The book is written so beautifully. It will give you a modicum of control in a horrible, out of control time. It will help you to know that grief is not linear. There is no right way. There is only your way.

You will also learn how deal to deal with those around you in their grief, and how to deal later when you begin to emerge into the world and have to tell total strangers about your loss. It is full of the resources that Sandy found most helpful for her and her family as they went through the worst that can happen.

It is a perfect book, written with love, knowledge, deep understanding, compassion and kindness.

I am bursting with pride for my dear, best friend Sandy. I have watched her come out the other end of a grief that would cause some people to just give up. She is brave, wise and always available to others who are in the throes of this horrific pain.

She still has moments of sadness but she lives her life from a place of joy and peace. She has been a wonder to watch and an inspiration to me.

My hope for you is that this book will guide you through to that place of peace as well. I send each of you who read this book, hope for peace and healing during this most gut-wrenching time.

I send you love,

Melissa Gilbert
Wife, Mother, Actress, Producer, Director, Activist,
New York Times best selling author

ONCE UPON A TIME I HAD A FAIRY TALE LIFE

"Change can happen at any time, but transition comes along when one chapter of your life is over and another is waiting in the wings to make its entrance."
-William Bridges, author of **The Way of Transition**

One thing is certain; nothing can ever be counted on to remain the same. When you try too hard to hold onto a time or a person or a feeling, it seems to be the very moment you are forced into transition, and it changes you, forever.

I remember the bliss of walking the Red Carpet at the Emmys when my husband was nominated as writer/producer for a show called **Beauty and the Beast.** The CBS television series was a modern-day fairy tale starring Linda Hamilton as the Beauty, and Ron Perelman as the Beast.

I thought of the years David and I envisioned the possibility of this very day. The night was so alive, radiating excitement, expectation, glamour, and beauty. It represented an achievement indeed, but enchanting nights like these often veil the common thread of human experience. It's hard to imagine sometimes, but these are real people with real lives, sometimes filled with joy, and sometimes, great tragedy.

We had a lot to be grateful for, but working in the entertainment industry wasn't always what it appeared to be. Sometimes we struggled to pay our bills, but we continued to stay focused on our goals and developed new storylines for new shows, hoping *the next one* would sell.

Our greatest achievement, however, was our growing family. Our two sons were at home on this special night, anxiously watching television for a glimpse of "Mom and Dad" on the Red Carpet.

The roundness of yet another child, a daughter, was hidden underneath the soft fabric layers of my gown.

I was caught up in the magic of fairy tales, believing that love conquers all, and everything I ever dreamed of could come true.

No one could have told me on that magical night, our family would soon be ripped apart by *the worst that could happen*.

Just five years later, our 16-year old son, Garrett, woke up with a fever and was dead the next morning. My beautiful, healthy, vibrant boy went from life to death in less than 24 hours by a lethal killer, bacterial meningitis.

It was on that tragic day, our castle walls tumbled to the ground.

Nothing evokes a more profound life change than loss, and nothing changes life like the death of a child.

It's often referred to as "the worst that can happen." When it's *your* child, you've unwillingly joined a group of people who know how it feels to have chapters of your life stripped away. Your future is changed forever, and your past will never, *ever* be the same.

Whether a child dies in the womb, in the early years, as a teenager, or as an adult, the pain that parents feel is the same. It's the deepest loss imaginable and *no one* is prepared.

How could we? We can't even bear the thought of it.

The death of a child is like an assault on everything you hoped for, dreamed of, believed in, and lived for. Everything is challenged, even your will to live.

At this point you have to make a choice: will you choose to go on living life, or will you remain trapped forever in a sad stifling world of bereavement?

How can you make a choice when you can't even breathe? Your focus is obsessively on the child you've lost. Your fairy tale is now set in a deep dark forest where grief is ominous and shrouds every bit of light in your life.

You know beyond a shadow of doubt, when you wake up in the morning, the sorrow will still be there, and it's another day, struggling to accept life with this cavernous hole in your heart.

Suddenly, those beautiful, joyful memories of your child's early years are painfully colored by the aura of loss. The death has changed every chapter of your book of life. The chapters are chaotic and out of sequence, because your child defied the natural order of life and left this earth before you.

You're now faced with having to create a whole new way of existing. You can't begin to believe that is even possible now . . .

3

But you will.

How? You ask, when grief is everywhere? It's like the air that you breathe, or the sky that is always there. You can't hide from it or escape it. As bereaved parents we feel life moving forward without us, and we begin to question how we can possibly go on. You search for the lost feeling of wholeness, a time when you were happy. There's no renegotiating, and there is no replacing what's been taken away. You are in the depths of despair. It strips away every part of your being, and all that you thought "was," is now gone forever.

Do you recognize yourself in these words and feelings? *Will you ever be happy again*, you ask?

Yes . . . you will.

I wrote this book as your guide, surrounding you like a comforting blanket woven with hope, love, and inspiration. Let me hold you and guide you. I've been through it, and I've survived.

You are *not* alone, I promise. There are many, like me, who have walked this path before you. It won't be easy to resurrect your life, but there are steps you can take to introduce peace, purpose, and joy back into your life. You *will* regain a quality of life that you can live with . . .

Yes . . . you will.

I promise that the lessons learned along the way will give you a better life than you are capable of imagining right now, because at this moment, you are in your deepest sorrow. You are in the middle of a grief storm.

Elisabeth Kübler-Ross, groundbreaking psychiatrist and pioneer in near death studies, introduced her theory of the five stages of grief in her book, **On Death and Dying**. You may recognize the stages:

- Denial
- Anger
- Bargaining
- Depression
- Acceptance

Each person's grief is unique, but you'll see yourself in these stages and the framework it provides in beginning to accept life with loss.

Through the process of recognizing my own Five Stages of Grief, I stumbled onto the path of a sixth stage. I call it *Resilience.*

At some point I realized resilience was my *only* option. I could not let the quality of life die around me. I had to be very much alive for my husband and living children. And I owed it to my beautiful boy, Garrett. He wouldn't want our family destroyed by his death.

He did not die in vain. Rather, he died and I was forced to find resilience and use it as a platform to resurrect myself. I had to form a new relationship with my son. I could no longer hold him in my arms, but in his death, it did *not* mean the end of my relationship with him.

In Worden's **Tasks of Grief,** the first task is to accept the reality of the loss intellectually, emotionally, and spiritually.

I know this is hard to imagine in the depths of your sorrow, and I can't tell you convincingly that you'll be just fine as you navigate the course of acceptance. There's no doubt this loss has changed your life forever, but how you choose to live the rest of your life is going to be your personal challenge. You'll have to learn to find balance in allowing time for your tears, and time to fully function in life.

The second task of grief is to identify, experience, and work through the pain. Easier said than done.

Just when you think you are healing, grief rears up and tries to shut you down.

Grieving is never linear. The tears and sorrow may return with a vengeance. This is all part of the process. However, as you begin to heal, the stages may not last as long or feel as dark.

Every day will be a myriad of emotions. You wake up in the morning, and for a brief moment, you believe your loss was a terrible dream, and then it hits you. It's the harsh, cold, frightening reality that you are waking up to your new life, one that no longer holds your child in it.

And the healing begins again and again, until one day you won't wake up with that thought. This is Worden's third task of grief: adjusting to a new life and environment without your beautiful child.

Once you're able to accept this new life, you'll move to the fourth task, re-directing the emotional focus away from your child, and compartmentalizing the emotion and devastating loss, in order to make room for the future and relationships it holds in promise.

You're not alone. I've walked this path before you . . . so have many others . . . and we're still standing. If you're just beginning your healing path, it may seem as though the road is so very long. It did to me too. I never saw the shred of possibility of seeing "happy" around the next bend.

What I *did* see, was one person that came to me on the day my son died, and he said, "This happened to me and my wife, and I promise, you *will* be okay. It's a long process. But you *will* heal. I promise."

And I have.

Healing doesn't mean you'll never feel the pain. Healing doesn't mean you'll forget and no longer feel the depths of despair. Healing doesn't mean that you won't ever long for your child.

Healing means you'll find acceptance as a choice, and your light will shine again. You'll feel the presence of loss always, but you'll find a way to fit it into your life instead of it taking control of your life.

In fact, you'll miss the tears erupting from the deepest part of bereavement, from the very core where love lives in your heart. One day those tears will no longer be needed, but available when you want them.

It was often hard to let go of mourning. It's emotion borne out of love that's so intense you can feel it in every cell of your body. Your tears are like holding him in your arms again. It's the sweet spot of connection between parent and child. Even in death, the bond can't be broken.

Grief still comes in waves for me . . . more a sense of weariness than an intense stabbing pain. It was surprising to discover, no matter how great my loss, or how deep my grief, the world doesn't stop. In fact, it intensifies. I wanted each day with my living children and husband to count. I wanted *my life* to count.

I will be navigating the stepping-stones of bereavement with you. I learned from my own tragic loss that you have two choices. To live or just exist. I chose to live, and I offer that choice to you.

Within the pages of this book, I'll take you through the process of regaining a quality of life you can live with. It will give you permission to cry . . . and to laugh. It will take you by the hand and teach you to be resilient. It will teach you the circle of life, and will hold you up, until you find your own strength again.

Bishop T.D. Jakes said, *"It is the breaking of life that produces the blessings of life."*

How difficult that may seem to comprehend at this dark hour. How do you find blessings after losing your child? Well . . . you don't. Blessings find you.

Grief is not a life sentence. Grief is a life passage. The word "passage" is "the act or process of moving through." It may seem impossible to move through *this passage* in the midst of despair.

Well-meaning family and friends will offer you their love and support in the best way they know how. They try to tell you that you'll be fine some day, but they can't possibly know what it's like to lose a child.

But I do . . . because I, too, lost my beautiful child.

I'm offering you all that I know, to give you *hope*. This is not a book on how to stop grieving; rather, it's a guide to accepting the reality, releasing the pain, and learning a new way of life, one day at a time.

There are others who need you to *live* again. As you open your heart to healing and allow others to love you through the process, you'll discover your heart will begin to heal.

Yes, your child died and the *only* choice you have is to walk the path of bereavement.

But you are not alone.

Together, we will acknowledge your loss, work the steps, and find renewal. *Together* we will restore hope and possibility. *Together*, we will reclaim your life.

I promise.

BEGINNING YOUR JOURNEY

Each section offers insight and stories borne from my own journey of recovery, along with extensive research, my volunteer work helping other parents and siblings through bereavement, and insightful therapists who enlightened me on this quest to discover the stepping stones to learning how to live life with such a tragic loss.

You may find shades of yourself within these chapters, uncovering feelings, fears, sorrows, and truths you're discovering. At the end of each section is a series of exercises. I call them "**Stepping Stones**" to your recovery. I urge you to begin them . . . at least promise yourself that you will begin the journal.

By participating fully in the exercises is the quickest road to finding balance and recovery in your life.

In this workbook style format the odyssey of grief shifts from one of passive submission into active recovery. While reading the story and working the steps you will actively pursue reclaiming your joy, and ultimately, you will triumph.

If you find you're not ready to take on an exercise in the order that it's listed, just skip it and move to an exercise that you'd like to complete. Just reading about it will offer awareness and benefit healing. You'll positively benefit either way.

This work is for you. Know that I am just like you. I, too, lost a child and I have survived. What's important now, is that you begin *your* crusade, taking the first step *now*, on the path of recovery.

That's all that matters.

THE LONG AND WINDING ROAD

Say to yourself, "I promise I will honor my child by healing."

Since the loss of your child, no doubt you've been in a haze of emotions. You've surrendered to the hold it has on you, yet you look for a way to release the shackles of sorrow. You're frightened that you will always feel this way.

To quote the amazing Beatles, "It's a long and winding road . . ." Indeed, and there's a way to set forth on the path of grief recovery, no matter how reluctant or disbelieving you are. It just takes one step to start your journey.

That one step begins with the process of writing. The very nature of writing opens the brain and allows for a combination of thoughts and emotions to form the words you put on paper. And then, it releases them.

It's a way of emptying your sorrow from the well of your mind, and pouring your tears as ink onto paper. And . . . for a little while, you can let your thoughts and emotions rest.

Then, an amazing thing begins to happen. You see *hope* rise up within your words.

"But, how can I?" you ask. "I'm not a writer."

It doesn't matter. The words aren't important, but your feelings are. Even if you begin by writing one line, your mind will send the words to your pen and they will flow onto paper.

It was an effort for me, too. When I began my grief journey, I could only write: *"My son died and my life will never be the same."*

The next day, I wrote a paragraph, and each day after that I found the words came more easily. There's no magic secret. Just pick up a pen and begin with one word or one sentence.

Writing helps with clarity, and monitors the grieving process. Right now, you are *in the beginning* stages where your grief is raw and unfiltered.

The word "grieving" comes from an ancient word meaning "heavy" and defines the feeling that accompanies loss.

There's another reason for this journal. It's going to be your resource guide, much like a compilation of a memory book, an address book, a scrapbook, a quote book . . . a book of *hope*.

In the next chapter, you'll discover how you will use it as your **Lifeline** (the supporting group of people we will be creating). It's also your daily planner (very important!), a place to list soothing foods and recipes, poetry, quotes, photos, pressed flowers, and possibly even drawings of a garden or sacred space you'll be creating.

My journal documented my deep sadness, my weakened spirit, and my empty heart, but it also held the secrets to my healing path, dreams I'd had, and evidence that my son was still with me. Then, something shifted. I began to write about more than just my sorrow. I began creating a written vision board for reclaiming my life.

I treasure the journals I kept during the mourning of my son because I had thoughts that, to this day, astound me. It illuminated the development of my beliefs, my renewal, and my incredible "will" to survive. It will provide a framework to monitor your resilience. Someday, *you too*, will look back on your journal and be astonished at how far you've come.

The process of writing is a natural demand on the brain that awakens the ability to recognize how you are, emotionally. This allows chemicals and "feel good" hormones to fuel your brain.

Dr. James Pennebaker, a social psychologist at the University of Texas, is considered one of the pioneers in writing therapy. His work confirms that writing your deepest thoughts and feelings is a tool for healing and reclaiming a quality of life after loss.

When we begin to translate our thoughts and emotions into language on paper, we detach it from our brain in order to write it down. This gives us a means to be an observer and contemplate what we've been through. It's a tool of expression, and for me, it often took the place of tears. Don't worry about your spelling, grammar, or handwriting. This is for you and no one else.

It gives you a safe place to:

- **Tell the truth about what you're feeling**
- **Reflect**
- **Notice emotions and reactions**
- **Ask questions**
- **Be angry**
- **Be sad**
- **Reveal weakness**
- **Search for serenity**
- **Reveal hope and write your vision for the future**

It's the power of written expression that can allow you to take a step away from living it . . . to observing it. It's a way of clearing out of your brain. It will become your living textbook in the healing process.

In a way, you're downloading your life, putting it in a file, and adding to the possibility and mounting evidence that future files will some day offer you peace and happiness.

Spend at least 10 minutes every day on your journal. Set aside the time, and make it consistent. It should be non-negotiable, like eating healthy food, and getting exercise.

People like to say, "Time heals all wounds." That saying may not feel true for a parent who's lost a child. I would like to offer, however, it's what you do with that time that can escalate healing and acceptance of your loss.

Be patient with yourself.

Your healing begins today . . . not tomorrow, not a week from now. The quicker you take action, the less fallout you'll have in your life.

Losing a child can take its toll on relationships and families. Embarking on a path to healing is the protection your family needs in this tragic time. They are all wondering if life will ever be the same. Offer them the gift of beginning your *own* healing journal, and their healing will follow.

Start with this simple journal exercise and soon, you will have confirmation that you *are*, in fact, on the path (even it's small steps) to surviving this terrible tragedy, one day at a time.

Stepping Stones: The Journal and the Journey

You will be working with a journal/workbook. Think of this tool as a sacred, non-negotiable part of your process. As time passes you'll come back to it and you'll be able to reflect on the time that's passed and witness the change and recovery you've experienced.

Remember that grieving is a very fluid process, so the responses, feelings, and ideas prompted by the exercises will constantly be changing over time.

- **Purchase a journal/workbook.** These will be used to store your private thoughts, reflections, and experiences, as well as organize your life from this day forward. Within these pages you'll discover your lifeline to active recovery along with an expression of private thoughts.

- **You can insert pictures or mementos of your child** inside the front cover of your journal/workbook, so you always have your favorite images available.

- **Make a commitment to working for a bit of time each day** on some process related to your loss and recovery. Journal just a sentence, if that's all you can do, but stick to it.

- **Structure your life in your journal.** Use it to schedule appointments, write lists of things to remember, make plans, and many other activities outlined in the upcoming chapters.

- **Many people prefer to write on a computer.** I did both. I wrote in a journal, but I wrote letters to my son on the computer. I urge you to commit to the written journal first. The act of writing with a pen allows thoughts to flow from your brain, and uninterrupted by things like spell check, emails coming in, and auto formatting.

- **On the first page of your journal write boldly:**

My child died, and this is the beginning of my new life, learning how to live with this loss. I promise I will honor my child by healing.

YOUR LIFELINE:
FRIENDS AND FAMILY

*In nature, when a female elephant is sick or wounded, the other
females form a circle around her. They protect her, nurture her,
and watch over her until she is strong enough to stand on her own.*

The day after your child died, you were probably surrounded by
friends and family wanting to help you in any way they could.
Take note of those people in your life, because they will be your
Lifeline.

Melissa Gilbert is one of those friends. In fact, she's my best
friend. You may have watched her grow up as the young actress
who played Laura Ingalls on "Little House on the Prairie," or the
many movies she did as an adult. We've shared good times and
the saddest of times. She said of our friendship:

*"What doesn't kill you makes you stronger. It's so true. My best
friend and I have talked about this and we boiled it down. We came
up with the idea that life is like a pearl necklace. In between each*

pearl is a knot. Without the knots, the pearls would fall away. The pearls are the good times in life—births, celebrations, marriages, and joys . . . the knots are the hard times, but they hold it all together. You can't have one without the other."

My son died a week before Christmas and Melissa was there for me. I remember speaking with her the day before Christmas Eve. I was overwhelmed with the thought of wrapping presents for my living children. I knew it was important to still have Christmas morning, no matter what. I wanted them to keep their child heart intact. It would be a welcome break from sadness *if* we could pull it together.

I called Melissa on the phone, "I can't do this," I cried.

"Yes, you can, because I'll help you," she replied. She arrived at my house 20 minutes later with wrapping paper, scissors, and tape.

It was the perfect way to prepare for *this* Christmas. Melissa and I sat outside on the patio with hot cups of tea and Christmas cookies. As we cut paper and tied bows, we recalled stories, laughed at some of Garrett's funniest moments, cried a few tears, but ultimately all the gifts were wrapped, and my living children could look forward to Christmas morning.

As unimaginable as it may seem to celebrate Christmas just 6 days after my son died, I discovered that carrying on with tradition and routine can sometimes give you hope that you can learn to live with your loss.

At first it was awkward to accept help. I was always the one who wanted to help others, and it was difficult to comprehend I was powerless. I needed their strength.

At the time, I didn't realize what I was giving to my friends in allowing *them* to help *me*. My friends felt needed.

Allow your friends the gift of being of service during your time of grieving. They are your **Lifeline**.

From this point forward, your relationships will define themselves through this great tragedy. Your friends and family will look to you in awe as you tread the treacherous waters of sorrow. As odd as this may seem, you will actually be the barometer as to how they continue their relationship with you.

They will find it difficult to watch your pain, and want so badly to help and find the right words to ease your pain. Speak freely of your child and this will allow them to feel safe in talking with you. This allows you to be held in a compassionate circle of love. You see, it's human nature to feel compassion and empathy.

In this exercise you will make lists of people you can count on. You will define their strengths and gently remember their weaknesses. Some of them will know exactly how to support you and love you.

Some will only know how to cook for you, or clean your house. Some will help with your children, and their activities. Some will sleep on your couch when you need them.

By creating this list, you'll know exactly who to call, and for what. Your family and friends are the ones who will give you their strength when you can't find it within yourself.

In nature, when a female elephant is sick or wounded, the other females form a circle around her. They protect her, nurture her, and watch over her until she is strong enough to stand on her own.

You really do have a circle of friends and family who are ready to do that for you. You have to let them embrace you in the only way they know how, and forgive them for their indiscretions and feelings of helplessness.

Reach out, and they will encircle you through your time of healing.

In this stepping stone exercise, we will identify your circle of support, their strengths, and *your* needs.

Stepping Stones: Your Lifeline List

From an organizational perspective it helps to do this early in your recovery process. If you find it challenging, ask a friend or family member to do it with you.

- **Create your Lifeline. In your journal/workbook make a list of names** of all the people in your life that you know can offer support at this time.
- **Learn to ask and accept help.** Remember, people really do want to help. They will be your Circle of Angels who can hold you up until you can stand on your own.
- **Note the people you can ask for logistical help** with household tasks or childcare. These are people who can take the role of offering practical support. Categorize your list by attaching "names" to "needs," such as:

    - Meals, packing lunches, etc.

- Grocery shopping
- Errands
- Laundry and changing linens
- Child care
- Picking up children from school and activities
- Appointments
- Banking, post office
- People at work who can help you during this transition
- Financial counselor
- Legal guidance, if necessary

- **Add new names as people reach out to you** or as you meet new people. This list of social support can give you a powerful sense of safety and caring during your darkest hours. It will help your family feel cared for, too.

- **Find a Support Group.** Consider contacting a group like "Compassionate Friends." (Specializing in parents who've lost children. View resources at www.SandyPeckinpah. com) and/or a therapist who specializes in grief. This may be too overwhelming in the beginning, but a few weeks down the road, try thinking about it again.

Honoring the Life Not Fully Lived

The Service and Burial

If you've already completed this difficult step of your loss, you may skip to the next chapter. Or, you may choose to read this chapter as a point of reference in healing.

*The most important thing to remember is that you did the best you could. Have **no** regrets about the decisions you made in the service and burial of your child.*

Planning a service for your child is beyond the scope of any parent's imagination. And yet, it's an important part of the grieving process. You deserve a service that represents your child's life, and a starting point for grief recovery.

Your mind is in shock and yet you are suddenly asked to plan this monumental event for possibly hundreds of people. How do you do it?

You just do the best you can and ask others to help you with the rest.

The starting point for me was in asking my pastor to conduct the service. If you don't participate in organized religion, enlist a few people from your circle of friends that can help you organize the service.

Your pastor or designated friend will want to meet with you to discuss your thoughts on how you want your child's life represented. Churches typically have guidelines for planning the service.

The purpose of the service is to provide a caring, supportive environment in which your friends and family gather to recognize the death of your child. It's a time to share thoughts and feelings. It's a safe place to express pain and be with people who care. It's a time when people surround you to help you through this passage.

Look at your list of support (from the previous chapter) and select a friend or family member to go with you to this meeting. **Take your journal/workbook with you.** Your mind cannot remember much right now, so ask your friend to write down all that is necessary to plan. This friend can then delegate the logistics and planning that needs to be done.

If you don't use a pastor or church head, find a person who can act as the anchor, someone who is comfortable speaking in front of people. He will be in charge of the "welcome introduction" and introduce the speakers and any other planned event such as music and video tributes.

My husband and I asked several friends to speak. If they didn't feel they could, they recommended other people.

Look for special things in your child's life that will bring their spirit into the service.

These can be photos blown up poster size (as we did with Garrett's football photo). They can be school papers, letters, and meaningful music. Look for things that define your child's spirit.

My son loved the **Grateful Dead** band. His favorite song, "Sugar Magnolia," was played at his service. Ask a friend to compile a Playlist of music that represents your child.

On the altar, we displayed Garrett's old wooden high chair (passed down from his Grandfather), along with his tiny first pair of cowboy boots. We hung the Superman cape I'd made for him when he was just three years old.

If your child died in the womb or as an infant, find ways to honor them with poetry, music, and art. You had dreams for raising your child. **Your loss is as great as those of us who watched our children grow.**

"Before I formed you in the womb I knew you; Before you were born I sanctified you."—**The Bible, Jeremiah 1:4** (NKJV)

There will be people who will want to speak, and people who are at a loss for words, but wish they could say something. Those that speak are offering a great tribute to your child and the people attending. For those that can't find the words to say but want to speak, offer them letters to read, or poetry, anything that represents your child.

If the location of your service has a screen and video capabilities, you may want to consider having someone put together a video commemorating your child's life. This is optional and can also be done later and distributed to friends and family individually.

You have so much to think about, it may be overwhelming to attempt to put together something of this magnitude before the service. If you decide to do it, peruse your **Lifeline List** for someone who knows video production, and delegate the task to him/her.

If you have young children, should they attend the service? Your decision about this is a personal one. It involves evaluating your children emotionally, your spiritual beliefs, and how you feel it will impact your children. Your children aren't in a position to understand what they are choosing or what is best for them. You can certainly ask your pastor, therapist, and people you trust. Ultimately it's your judgment call. Once you've made the decision, have no regrets.

Be prepared on the day of the service to feel overwhelmed with emotion. Not only do you have to get yourself ready, but, depending on your situation, you may also have to help your partner and your other children get ready too.

I found it so difficult the morning of the service. I was running late because going to the service meant my child was really dead. Every time I thought I was emotionally ready, I would cry uncontrollably.

Melissa and her husband Bruce arrived at our home to drive us. She took me by the hand and never let go.

I was astounded at the number of people sitting at the church, waiting for us to arrive. As we took our seats and looked at the altar of Garrett's things, it became real.

Reverend Carpenter began. "Garrett was an extraordinary kid! So says everybody who met him, and got to know him. His sudden death is as tragic an event as ever could take place. I have watched as people who do not even know the Peckinpahs, break down and cry at the news."

And this is how it is when you lose a child. It's massive empathy surrounding you whether you realize it or not, because the loss of child is truly the worst that could happen. Take the time to feel it in your heart. People want to be there for you.

Rev. Carpenter's words continued. "Another blessing is that he was home, in his own bed, with his family."

Yes, I thought, and the last words I spoke to him were "I love you, honey."

The next speaker, Sally Jordan, spoke of her hours as Garrett's teacher, exploring the world of literature. She spoke of Garrett's favorite Christmas story, Truman Capote's "A Christmas Memory." The book had such impact on Garrett, he considered being a writer.

Jack Scalia read a beautiful letter from Garner Simmons. Gar and his wife Sheila were a part of our lives since interviewing us for a book Gar was writing about David's legendary Uncle Sam in the 70's. Gar's urging and his inspiration was the reason David and I came to Los Angeles to begin a career in film and television.

"Remember," Garner wrote, "there was not just one Garrett Peckinpah. There were two. The handsome boy, who was with us too briefly, but who lit up our lives, may be gone, but the other . . . the true Garrett Peckinpah-is the one we carry in our hearts, forever youthful and alive."

Forever young. My boy will be 16 years, three months, and ten days . . . forever.

Melissa got up from beside me, squeezed my hand and took the podium. She looked straight at David and me. "How do I do this? What do I say?" she choked back tears.

I started to cry.

"I don't know how," she said as she bowed her head. She described the Garrett she knew. "Charming, funny, intelligent, loving, compassionate, stubborn, giving, handsome, athletic, ambitious, devoted, kindhearted, strong, understanding, generous, affectionate, gifted, concerned . . ."

She punctuated her next thought. "There are not enough words to describe the light of Garrett! He was the child all parents dream of having, that all children want for a brother. He was my friend. I honestly believe that he was just too good for us."

She was right. I always said Garrett was an old soul. Everyone said it.

I never thought, however, that it meant his life would be shortened because he was born *knowing*. Is that the way it works? We are born with a curriculum of lessons in life. When we're done, we graduate, life is over.

Melissa took her seat beside me.

Bruce stood up and walked to the podium. He began reading the letter Garrett had written to me in early December.

"Dear Mom,

I'm sitting here remembering the past moments and years of my life, thinking about my attitude, my perspective, and my feelings and emotions . . .

"*The only thing I can conclude about my life from sixth to tenth grade is that I never allowed myself to be who I really am. It seems that I was always trying to be cool, funny, or any other way that might please other people. What other people thought about me was more important than what I thought about myself.*"

Could he have known, somehow, that this would be read at his own memorial service? Did his soul know? This letter was his life and the transformation he had in the last few months.

It was the perfect tribute . . . and he had written it himself.

Bruce's powerful voice read each word of this letter that documented Garrett's life better than any of us could have. He continued . . .

"*I would buy clothes only after I figured out what other people would think. I was obsessed with my physical appearance. My hair had to be perfect. I had to have the clearest complexion and the coolest clothes. For me, my appearance became more than an obsession.*

"*At first, I really liked going to a public high school. It gave me a chance to be free, to feel like a real high school student. I was somewhat shy during the first few weeks, but I was still happy just to be there. I literally left my old friends behind. I was tired of that life, that unhappiness. Soon enough, I began to make many friends and acquaintances at my new school. But I began to once again become obsessed with my appearance. I tried desperately to find some sort of image, some kind of look. I didn't seem to attract girls' attention.*"

"During my freshman year, my grades were decent. That summer I went to the Orme Summer Camp for my third year in a row. That summer, in particular, showed me a hint of my real personality, my real image. I was popular! I went out with the most beautiful girl in camp; I made people laugh! I was just being myself for the first time".

"With that, I started my sophomore year (back at public school). Almost instantly I lost all my confidence and pride that I had finally found at a small summer camp in Arizona."

Then the bomb dropped: four D's on my first report card. I had never received a D . . . much less four of them. My schoolwork was pitiful, along with my self-motivation and drive. This crushed my parents to see their son ruining his future. For this, I cannot, and will never forgive myself."

"The worst part was that I didn't know why my grades fell and my motivation disappeared. I know now that it was my obsession with social acceptance . . . ."

Garrett had really struggled. I'd sit in his room trying to help him with homework. He was smart, but his focus was just somewhere else.

Bruce continued reading.

"I finished the year an academic reject. I was forced by my parents to attend summer school . . . but it was the same place I had found myself in the years past.

But this was different-this is school-I reasoned. It turned out that this would be the most important summer of my life.

I rediscovered how to study, how to do homework, how to be a student . . .

"I got two A's that summer at Orme. The letter continued on with revelations about himself and his education.

We decided together that he could continue at Orme for high school.

"The first major event that changed my thinking about myself was joining the football team.

"In my first game I scored a touchdown and caught a crucial pass at the end of the game. Those two plays alone might well have changed my attitude right there. I could do it. No doubt. I had done well. Football that season gave me confidence in myself as never before. But that was nothing compared to my report card for the first quarter. Three A's and two high B's! Honor Roll!"

"I had done it. I had made myself proud, and I knew my parents would be proud . . ." Bruce's voice shook as he continued reading Garrett's letter.

Suddenly, I was Garrett Peckinpah. I was a person who knew myself, and others knew me . . ."

I heard muffled cries throughout the church. I heard a few notes on the guitar, and then my friend, Nan began singing Amazing Grace.

So Garrett had done it . . . he had written his own tribute . . . and when he died, he was at the top of his game.

Stepping Stones: The Service in Tribute to Your Child

The funeral or memorial service can be an overwhelming task. There are so many decisions to be made. The first thing to do is **ask people to help**. It's the only way you can get through it.

- **If you are a member of the church, ask a family member or friend to help you** with making and attending the appointment with the pastor.
- **The pastor will guide you with a sample service.**
- **If you are not connected to a church, ask your friends to help you organize your own service.** Choose one friend who can act as the anchor and introduce the line up of those that will be speaking, reading, and singing.
- **If you choose to do the service where your child will be buried, then establish a meeting** at the funeral home. The director will be able to guide you.
- **Have friends from your Lifeline List help you** with photographs and mementos you want to display at the service.
- **Decide on the music or assign a friend to organize for you.** You may have friends who want to sing or play music, or simply a friend who can put together a **Playlist** on a **CD**.
- **Take your videos to a friend who will organize and decide how to put together a brief remembrance on video.** You can do a longer version down the road, but for now, you are having to assemble everything very quickly. If you don't have a way of viewing a DVD in the church, then it can be played at your home after the service.
- **Is there one special picture of your child that represents his life the best?** Ask a friend to take it to a printer and have it blown up poster size and mounted for display on an easel.

- **Choose other mementos that represent your child.** A favorite drawing, an English paper, or a letter. All of these can be blown up into posters to become part of the story of your child's life.
- **If your child died in the womb or as an infant, find ways to honor them** with poetry, music, and art
- **Decide who will speak and decide the order with which they will speak.** Give that list to the pastor.
- **Assign several friends for letting people know the time and date of the service.** They can send out cards, emails, make phone calls . . . anyway that is necessary to do it in the shortest amount of time because services come very shortly after the death.
- **Typically there is a gathering in your home or banquet hall after the service.** Choose where that will be and ask one or two people to organize that for you. This is not the time for you to be cooking or shopping. This is a time to really let others take over for you.
- **Ask your closest friend to guide and support you on this tragic, difficult day.** Your spouse can't really do it. They are grieving deeply with you. They need a friend to help them, too.

Lastly, years down the road, I really don't remember many details of how my son's memorial service was organized so beautifully. I just know it all came together because people stepped in to help. This usually happens because people care so much.

Stepping Stones: Your Child at Rest

Another huge stepping stone is deciding how to handle your child's burial. You'll need to meet with a funeral home to make the decisions about whether you'll bury your child, or if cremation is appropriate. It is your decision and your belief system that will help you decide.

Please be prepared with how difficult this is.

Ask a friend or a pastor to research burial options with you.

- **It's difficult to decide where to lay your child to rest, and how.** Have a friend go with you to the cemetery to make decisions on burial and caskets. Some may choose to scatter ashes. In that case, you will need to order the cremation.

- **Stay focused on the immediate task.** The funeral home may try to sell you extra plots, stones, all kinds of things. It will be easier if you can just ask them to stay focused on what is right for your child at this moment. You're not emotionally stable enough to make decisions right now. Concentrate on what is absolutely necessary.

When the funeral and burial are over, you'll remember parts of it and some of it will be a fog. **Make peace the moment you leave the service and bury your child . . . you did the best you could and that effort was beautiful in it's grace.**

LEARNING TO TALK ABOUT THE DEATH OF YOUR CHILD

"By taking the first step, (in talking about your child), the danger is averted of the awkward pause that could last a lifetime."
-Harriet Sarnoff Schiff, Author of ***The Bereaved Parent***

The night following the death of my son, throngs of people came to our home. I couldn't eat or drink. I walked out to the front yard and saw the Christmas lights dangling from the eves. I never finished the task of hanging them the night Garrett was sick. It had been more important to sit with him in his room, wiping his brow.

December 19th . . . the saddest day of my life. Darkness came quickly. People mulled about fixing dinner. I attempted to carry on conversations but really couldn't make sense of what I was trying to say.

I suddenly felt light headed and lay down on the couch and closed my eyes.

Someone stroked my head. It was Sally Jordan, my writing teacher and friend. Her only daughter had died the summer before. I don't remember ever talking with her about it, but I must have. Or . . . I must have avoided it.

"I know how you feel," she said.

Yes. She did.

"You'll find the pain unbearable at times," she continued.

"It's unbearable now, Sally," I replied. "I can't stop thinking. It won't stop. He's everywhere. He runs in my mind. The memories won't stop."

"I know, she replied, "Your brain is processing. You'll never stop missing him, but the times you feel the intensity of the sorrow will lessen. You'll go on . . . life will get better."

"What do I say to people?" I asked, "They'll see me as such a tragic person."

"No, she said. "They will see you as a triumphant person."

Sally helped guide me into the world of talking about my dead son. She said, "Tell the world before they tell you. When you go to the grocery store and they ask how you are, tell them, 'I'm sad. My son died and I'm having to adjust to it.'"

In the beginning, I did just that. I told the lady at my dry cleaners, the woman behind the counter at my favorite Italian deli. I told the gardener, my banker, the guy that worked out next to me on the treadmill at the gym . . . just about everybody that I had daily or weekly contact with. I was armed and ready so that I was emotionally in control of my conversations.

This may be contrary to what you might think. Is it selfish? Does it make others sad? It often does, but it can be a gift and a reminder to the world that loss can happen when you least expect it. It tells them "Treasure what you have, now."

The most important thing is that it's helping *you* adjust and heal. Most people responded with compassion, "I'm so sorry." Some pulled from the passel of grief responses such as "he's in a better place, or he's with the angels now." And some didn't say anything at all and continued talking about the weather.

People don't know what to say to a mother who has lost a child. But what they say is not the important point here. This exercise allows *your* spirit and wounded heart to hear "my child died" over and over again in order for *you* to adjust to it, and ultimately find acceptance.

Gina, the wonderful social worker that heads up grief groups for children experiencing loss, said it's important to tell the story again and again, because it helps your mind fully comprehend and accept the reality.

It's not that it grows numb to the tragedy, it's that it compartmentalizes it so you have better control. She also stresses the importance of using the word "died" more frequently than "lost" or "passed way."

Your child isn't "lost," your child didn't "pass" somewhere. Your child died. As tragic as that sounds, it's exactly what happened.

People usually don't ask how, but some will. Be prepared with an answer. You don't have to tell the exact truth if you don't want to.

For parents who lose a child to suicide or a brutal death, it can be difficult to find the right words. Only *you* will know what those words are.

My friend's daughter had schizophrenia and took her own life. When asked about it, she would say, "My daughter struggled with mental illness, and we miss her."

Sometimes people will ask how your child died. Curiosity? Yes, but often their fear is what motivates them to ask. They don't want to believe that such a random tragedy could happen to their child. One friend said I saved her daughter's life, because at the onset of a sore throat and stiff neck, she remembered the details I gave her about Garrett. She didn't let the doctor write it off to the "flu." She insisted on more tests, and she was right, her daughter had meningitis. **In his death, my son saved her daughter's life.**

Are you beginning to realize the responsibilities you have as a parent who has lost a child? Hard to imagine when you are in the throes of grief, but your loss will have far reaching meaning to others. **It may just save a child's life.**

You will disarm people when you are able to talk about your child. My friends told me years later, they were relieved when I talked about Garrett. It's like "the elephant in the room." People know it's there but are afraid to acknowledge. When you speak first, it's a great relief to them, and it takes the pressure off of you.

As years go by, the need to tell your story will dissipate and then you can decide whether to talk about it at all.

My personal coach and friend, Bob Donnell, who tragically lost his three-year old daughter in a car accident says to evaluate the "relationship currency" with that person before revealing your story. Ask yourself, "Will I see these people again? Are they going to be involved in my life? Is it important they know?"

Often you'll be asked, "How many children do you have?" To this day, I still stumble on that question. Please don't feel guilty if you choose to acknowledge only your living children. I know my son lives forever in my heart. This is *your* survival story, and your answer will depend on how you feel at that moment.

Stepping Stones: Clarifying your Story & Sharing with Others

The following exercises will help you develop, adjust to, and tell your story.

- **Develop your sentence about the death of your child. Make it short, and complete.** Mine was this: "My oldest son Garrett died. He woke up with a fever and was dead the next morning of bacterial meningitis. It's been really hard."
- **Do you see how those few sentences tell them everything they need to know?** It makes it easier because they will want to know, but don't know how to ask. By being direct, you are avoiding the awkwardness of them trying to ask.

- **That last line "It's been really hard" or "I'm having to adjust," is really important,** because that gives them the line they need to say next, without stumbling. They can now say, "I'm so sorry. Yes it must be hard." This is not to protect them or be responsible for their feelings; it's to protect *you* and your emotional state. You are prepared.
- **Just keep working on it until it flows.**
- **As time goes by, the need to tell your story will lessen.** Then, you will only tell your story to those that are involved in your life in some way and have **earned the right to know.**

Stepping Stones: Sentence Completions

This exercise will help you in talking about your child. The grief process often leaves your mind overwhelmed, so this sentence completion exercise is designed to help you explore your memories and feelings in a more focused manner.

Find a quiet place where you can be alone and very comfortable. If you'd like, choose a beautiful outdoor space or a safe space such as your bedroom. Write the beginning of each sentence below, in your journal. Then reflect on it. Close your eyes, feel, and visualize how you'd like to complete the sentence in words. Finish the sentence in your workbook.

- **What I miss most about my child is . . .**
- **The hardest part of the day is . . .**

- **When I focus on how my body feels, I feel sadness (or anger) in . . .**
- **I feel angriest that . . .**
- **My biggest unanswered question is . . .**
- **Someone (or something) that gives me a lot of comfort is . . .**
- **I worry that . . .**
- **One beautiful memory of my child is . . .**

After you complete these sentences, share them with a friend, family member or therapist. The more you are able to talk about it, the quicker your body, mind, and spirit will begin to accept and heal.

THINGS PEOPLE SAY

*There <u>are</u> no adequate words for someone who has
lost a child . . . only the intention with which they
are spoken, and the love radiating from them.*

It's important to recognize that some of your friends will make
mistakes. They will say things like, "He's in a better place now."
And you will think, *What? How could you say that? The best place
for my child is in my arms!*

They will say, "Why don't we go to a funny movie, you need
to laugh." And you will think, *Laughter? That's the last thing I can
do. Don't you understand? The only emotion I can fathom right now
is sadness!*

They will say, "He's with the angels now." And you think, *But
he's not supposed to be with angels now, he's my beautiful boy. He
had his whole life to live!*

They will say, "God doesn't give you more than you can
handle," and you will say, "*Then let me die now, because I <u>cannot</u>
handle the death of my child.*"

Some people won't say anything at all, and later they will tell you, "Well, I didn't want to bring it up because I didn't want to remind you." And you think, *Do you really think it's in the back of my mind? The death of my child is in every cell, every thought, every breath I take, 24 hours a day. There is <u>never</u> a moment I forget.*

No, you never forget. You never get over it. You just learn how to live with it.

It's hard to imagine at this moment, but eventually you *will* regain a quality of life that includes happiness. But for now, it takes courage to face the day, and face people. Sometimes, you just have to wear a mask of being "okay."

I'm certain you've had comments already. I did from the very beginning. People want so badly to "fix you." And yet, there's nothing they can say to fix this.

How do you make peace with the things people say? I can only offer a verse from the Bible.

"Father, forgive them, for they know not what they do"
—The Bible, Luke 23:34, KJV

You must put aside the anger with the things people say and look, instead at the intention with which they were said. People don't want to see you suffer. Their intention is simply to try to "fix it" and make you feel better. Of course that's what they feel because they love you.

Your best response is to just say "thank you." Don't try to change them or educate them at this time. They are struggling to find words that will comfort you. If you offer them a hug, it will make *you* feel better and they will feel like they've done something right at a time when nothing feels right about your loss.

Perhaps some of your friends will take a step back from your life. There are many reasons they do. They fear saying the wrong thing and wounding you. They're afraid to be happy around you because they can't envision how you could possibly be happy again.

You may also find it difficult to listen to them talk about their children. When they do, you may feel your loss deeply, and maybe even feel anger. They have their child, and you do not. This may happen for years. It did for me. Just accept it, let it flow through you, and breathe the anger away.

Try not to judge people and the things they say. What happened to you is *their* worst nightmare. I know it's hard to imagine now, but down the road, they will marvel at your ability to go on. You will be a beacon of light. *You* will be the one they turn to, when it's their time to suffer a tragedy. No one is immune from tragedies in life. No one. It's part of the human experience on this planet.

Stepping Stones: When People Say the Wrong Thing

It's going to happen. Be prepared. You will hear so many wrong things people will say. Keep in mind why they are saying it, and what they are trying to do . . . make you feel better. When something very wrong comes out of their mouths, do the following:

- **Very simple, just breathe** and know their intention is to help you, not harm you.
- **Allow feelings of love to fill the awkward space.** Hard to imagine? Just think if it was *their* loss.
- **Respond by saying** "Thank You." Now is not the time to struggle with relationships nor is it the time to teach them how wrong they are.
- **A hug gives a physical connection of understanding.** If you are comfortable, offer one.
- **Again . . . Just breathe.**

Taking Care of
Yourself First

"There is so much love in your heart that you could heal the entire planet. But just for now let us use this love to heal you."
-Louise L. Hay, author of **You Can Heal Your Life**

Within a few days of Garrett's death, I lost 12 pounds, was exhausted by lack of sleep, and my eyes looked hollow and sunken. I found it difficult to eat or sleep. I stubbornly refused drugs and sleep aids.

When I fainted the day after my son died, I realized I hadn't eaten since the day before it all happened.

You've experienced a terrible shock and your system is rebelling. You either grimace at the thought of food, or you go the other way, and use food as comfort.

You may be drinking too much, or turning to drugs.

You're not able to track daily habits, and you're not sleeping at all or too much.

Where do you turn for help in this grief storm? This is where your **Lifeline** comes in.

My childhood best friend, Paula flew in from San Francisco to be with me the day after Garrett died. She has a beauty and a calm that I know I can count on. She has always been a constant in my life, since childhood. We traveled the world together in a show called "Up With People." There is something very powerful and soothing about shared history. It connects you forever.

Paula was a nurse. She recognized immediately what I needed. Because the doctors were uncertain of why Garrett died, we were on 24-hour watch for signs of illness.

Paula monitored how we ate, slept, and administered preventative medication.

I remember so clearly, waking up in the middle of the night, the children in sleeping bags surrounding our bed, and there was Paula with a tiny flashlight, examining our sleeping children for signs of rash or fever.

It makes me cry to this day, because she was our angel in the night. She protected us and made us feel safe in a time of great fear.

This is the importance of surrounding yourself and embracing the best friends you have. You are ravaged by such incredible loss, and your friends are there to hold you together.

Being physically healthy and nourished is imperative to your recovery, and we often overlook it, because our minds are obsessed with our child. You may not only forget to eat, but to bathe, to take vitamins or medications, or even brush your hair and teeth.

I'm so grateful I had a friend who held me accountable for exercise. Within a week of Garrett dying, Randi had me meet her at the gym to work out. I don't even know why I agreed. I arrived with dark sunglasses and tears in my eyes.

"I don't know if I can do this Randi," I said.

"That's why *I'm* here," she replied.

And we continued my work out for an hour. It proved to me the value in what is released by the brain when you exercise. I felt stronger, better, and the tears left about halfway through the workout. I wouldn't have done it without my friend forcing me out of the house.

Reach out to someone you know who will hold you accountable.

There are times in your recovery, when medication can be necessary. There are also nutritional options such as herbs, teas, and the right foods that can help you with your sense of wellbeing.

Talk with your doctor about the options that are best for you.

Be aware that your whole immune system is affected by bereavement. Studies have shown after someone suffers a traumatic shock, the immune system is compromised for months, even years after.

Take the time to acknowledge the importance of a healthy body right now. The following stepping stones will help you become aware of your immune system, your body, and your self-care.

Stepping Stones: Self-care

The process of grieving naturally causes dramatic changes to your appetite; sleep cycles, and physical health. It's likely that you'll have to be patient with some of these changes, but it's also important to note the effect they may have on your day-to-day functioning. As you keep a daily journal try to note and track some of the following trends and details:

- **Food is critical in keeping you healthy at a time when your immune system may be compromised by grief.** This is a time when your brain does not give you the correct information on when to eat and when not to eat. I went for days without food and never felt hungry. The opposite can happen too, in that you may feel like eating constantly to soothe.

- **In your journal/workbook, create a list of foods** that you love and you know you will eat, even if you've lost your appetite. Keep healthy options such as veggies and fruits close at hand. I choose to start every day with a nutritional shake. That way, I know I'm getting nutrition first thing in the morning. If you find you're not eating enough try making or purchasing fruit or vegetable smoothies, which may be easier to eat. This list will be available to those wanting to help prepare meals and grocery shop for you.

- **Track your sleep routines in your workbook.** Making an effort to regulate your sleep will be a key part of keeping your body and mind strong and resilient. If you're having difficulty sleeping use techniques from meditation and relaxation discussed in a later exercise. If your sleep is extremely disrupted or you're struggling with nightmares, consult your doctor about natural or medical sleep aids. Good rest is essential to your recovery.

- **Fuel your Body with Neuro-chemicals** No . . . you can't find them in pill form at the pharmacy, but you *can* manufacture them in your body. Exercise daily, even if it's just a walk around the block. **Start with a promise in your workbook to take a walk every day.** It will release "feel good" endorphins into the brain. These are crucial to your recovery. Being outside, experiencing nature, and a shower of sunlight help heal.

- **Consider other alternatives to calming your body like Yoga or "Tapping."** What is Tapping? Go to the resource section at www.SandyPeckinpah.com for information.

- **Do at least one body-soothing activity per week.** Massages, hot baths, facials, pedicures, and even using an all-over body lotion are ways you can show yourself and your body love and care. It's important to think of yourself with the same loving and comforting energy you would offer to a sick or struggling loved-one.

- **Use Color Therapy.** Wear yellow, blue, or a color that makes you feel good. Avoid the habit of wearing black while mourning. **Yellow** tends to be a color that gives an uplifting feeling. **Blue** is soothing. **Green** is the color of life and nature. **Violet** is peaceful and soothes anxiety. **White** brings balance and harmony.

- **Make your needs known to others.** Ask a friend to walk with you, have tea with you, or just listen to you. Your friends want to help.

- **Schedule an appointment with your doctor if you are having unmanageable feelings or habits.** Your doctor will want to know how you're sleeping, eating, and managing this difficult time. This is a time for absolute honesty. Let your doctor know if you are drinking, taking drugs, or have developed erratic eating behaviors.

The first step in your grief recovery is to take care of you.

PLAYLIST OF MEMORIES

Memories are not images of loved ones returning to
us. They are the spirits of loved ones visiting us.
—**Mark Nepo**, author, **The Book of Awakening**

On the night of Garrett's death, exhausted, I lay down on the couch and closed my eyes. I shut myself off. I wrapped myself into a ball and stored myself in a cocoon of sadness. I heard only the din voices from all of those who gathered to support us through this tragic day.

My brain suddenly came alive. Although in shock, I awakened a compartment of memories, long since forgotten. The projector in my brain was an endless Playlist of Garrett's life. It was as clear as if they happened yesterday. I saw him as a baby, crawling in front of the shiny brass chest, amused by his own image. I could hear his voice in my head when he first learned to talk. His first word, "kitty" sputtered from his lips in delight.

Then I saw him riding his Big Wheel, laughing and screaming at pretend traffic. I heard him call "Mom!" but this time in his 16-

year old voice echoing down the hall. I saw him reading to Julianne the night before he left for school just a few short months ago.

When once, these memories brought me joy, they now tortured me because I could only attach the meaning of loss to them. They ran non-stop in my brain. Where were these coming from? Every second, a new memory would bubble to the surface, one I thought I'd long forgotten. They'd play over and over inside my head. I wanted them to stop and yet I didn't.

That night, I came to the profound realization, my brain was a massive hard drive of thoughts and memories, and nothing, *absolutely nothing* is ever really forgotten.

I've talked to other grieving parents, and most had the same reaction.

The human brain doesn't forget. The energy in it is always functioning, and the shock of losing Garrett awakened my brain like an earthquake uncovering old ruins, to memories that had been long forgotten. They were all still there, every moment of his life with me, filed away, recalled through grief.

At first, the obsessive memories became a part of my life like breathing. I would have to consciously push them aside to answer a question or carry on a conversation. Even then, my friends recalled I would often blankly stare, and they knew I was remembering.

A few months down the road, the obsessive thoughts quieted a little. It takes time. Be kind to yourself, and acknowledge this is a phase. It may feel like you're losing your mind or your ability to function, but it is part of the grieving process.

Begin practicing re-framing the memory. When you have one, notice how you feel. Is it a happy memory and yet you feel sad? Try detaching the sadness and re-boot the memory with only the feelings of joy.

You learn to celebrate the times you had with your child. Those treasured memories are all you have. It's those memories that will be forming the new relationship with your child for the rest of *your* life.

When those memories arise in your mind, the spirit of your child visits in your heart, and that brings you peace.

I read in John Assaraf's book, **The Answer**, about a series of experiments done by the famous lie detector expert, Cleve Backster. He took white blood cells from the mouths of his subjects and cultured them in a test tube. One of his subjects was a World War II Navy gunner.

His cultured white blood cells were taken to a location seven miles away. The culture was connected to a lie detector. This Veteran was shown a movie, "The World at War," about the Japanese attack on Pearl Harbor. During the movie, there was a close up of a naval gunner shooting at enemy aircraft.

The man's face did not show his reaction, but *seven* miles away, the white blood cells forced the lie detector needle to jump violently! The cells reacted to the emotion of the Veteran who was *seven miles away*! An energy field that no one could really explain connected the man to his cells!

My God, do you have any comprehension of what this means to a mother who has lost a child? We're still connected! He was born from the cells of my body, and although we are physically separated, no one can ever take away our union of spirit, love, and energy. *No one, not ever.*

Love creates that connection too, because *love is energy.* My friend, Melissa Gilbert, was adopted. She says there's a deep, special connection between parent and child when parents choose to adopt. The bond forms in the powerful act of love by bringing a chosen child into your heart and care.

As you begin to live again and make new memories and stories for your life, the torment of the endless Playlist will subside. They will transition into the archives, and you will recall them when you want. Now, your focus needs to be on the present and how you will focus on life, not death, every single day.

Being able to quiet your mind will help you find peace. It may seem impossible at this time but you must take steps to find it. Begin with a one-minute meditation or prayer. You can even just refer to it as "quiet time" if you are struggling with your faith. We will discuss this struggle in another chapter.

The key is to expect nothing from meditation and prayer, and consistent use will give you everything.

Close your eyes and focus on your breath. Listening to your breath is one of the hardest things to do. Thoughts will come in, but just see the thought wrapped inside a cloud and breathe the thought away.

Keep doing it. This is like sweeping your mind's "hard drive." You are attempting to put those memories away in a file to access when you *want to,* and *not* when they are tormenting you.

Start with 1 minute of quiet, and go up to 5 if you like.

As difficult as this is, all of these steps are important because you have the rest of your life to live. Your only choice is to move forward, one day at a time.

Stepping Stones: Quieting the Mind

There are ways you can sidetrack the torment of the endless Playlist of memories. Know that this is normal and is part of your brain processing what has happened. Consider these techniques to help quiet your mind.

- **Learn how to sit in stillness, meditate.** Meditation calms the body and the mind. It begins with closing your eyes and focusing on breathing. If you have a thought come into your mind, say to yourself, "a thought," then, just wrap it in a white cloud, and breathe it away. Focus on breathing again. This will be difficult at first because of nonstop recurring thoughts about your child. Start with 3 minutes. This is the beginning of getting control of obsessive thinking.
- **Listen to meditative music or sounds as you fall asleep. Focusing on music will help clear the replay of thoughts and calm your brain.** If it bothers your partner, use earphones.
- **Do activities that involve thinking** such as reading, playing "Words With Friends" on your phone or iPad, or watching a movie.

- **Physical activities can help your brain function optimally.** If you can, sports that involve team efforts (so it demands your attention) are the best. Try tennis, basketball, golf, or even a class at the gym.
- **Re-frame your memories.** When you have memories of your child and you feel sadness because of the loss, try detaching the feeling of sadness. You picture the memory, take a deep breath, and imagine the sad cloud around the memory. Blow the cloud away when you breathe out. Then, "re-boot" the memory, with only joy attached.

THE VOICE OF FEAR AND RESENTMENT

"Death is not a failure and grieving is not a sign of weakness."
—**David Kessler**, author with **Elisabeth Kübler Ross, On Grief and Grieving**

Within weeks after my son's death, I was aware of another voice taking up residence in my head. It was the voice of fear. I became obsessive about my family's whereabouts, their health, and continually felt anxiety around the possibility of losing them at any moment.

I had little rituals I would quietly say when they left the house. "Come home safe!" I would say. Or: "be healthy!" as if, somehow, it surrounded them in a protective bubble wrap.

These thoughts lived in my head and tortured me every day. Grief counselors call it. "Magical Thinking." It's a part of mourning. It's obsessive behavior and I couldn't stop. I worried I was losing my mind. I didn't share it with anyone. I was too embarrassed.

I panicked every time my children were out of my sight. Sometimes I would drive to where they were, like school, Brownie meetings, or the playground nearby, just to get a glimpse of them safe and alive.

I would get up in the middle of the night to watch my children breathe. Just breathe. I would stare at them in the dark, not wanting to wake them. If it was too dark, I touched them to make sure they would move.

While they were at school, I worried: *Did I remind them to wash their hands before eating? Did I mention not to be around kids who are coughing? Did I tell them what to do if they started choking?*

I had this obsessive need to stay busy and organized. Usually I would do something mindless, because my mind was always on my loss.

I organized things like linen closets, cupboards, and the garage. One sleepless night I got up and organized my library of over 500 books. I cleaned each shelf, each book, and organized them according to author and genre. I was probably the only home library in Westlake Village who had a library organized with a Dewey Decimal System.

This was beyond anything I could try to fix myself. I finally found the courage to tell Melissa I was really struggling. She encouraged me to schedule an appointment with her therapist.

After beginning therapy, I realized I was experiencing post traumatic stress. We most often hear that term in conjunction with war veterans, but it relates to those of us who have suffered the tragedy and trauma of losing a child.

Therapy is also a good place to acknowledge feelings of resentment you may be having, particularly if your child unjustly died or was hurt by another human being.

I struggled with feeling inadequate as a mother. Irrationally, I thought, *If I was a good mother, he wouldn't have died.* This is a stage of grief recognized as "bargaining."

My son woke up with a fever the Saturday before Christmas. I took him to the doctor at 11:00 a.m. and the doctor diagnosed him with the Type A flu.

The doctor recommended, "Lots of fluids and ibuprofen to keep his fever down," he said. "He should be better in a few days."

At midnight, I called the doctor to tell him Garrett was really struggling with a migraine.

"That's part of this flu. Just keep his fever down and make sure he's staying hydrated."

I believed him.

I kissed Garrett goodnight and somehow in the middle of the night, his heart stopped.

In the morning, I went to his room to awaken him. I found him dead.

Even the doctor was in shock. The undiagnosed bacterial meningitis was so aggressive it attacked his entire body and killed him in 24 hours.

Could I have sued the doctor for a misdiagnosis? Possibly. Would it have made my loss any easier? No.

If you choose to go the route of a wrongful death lawsuit, I urge you to consider the mental anguish and the consequences. It's so very difficult.

If it's the only way you can manage the financial burden of medical bills and your future, please consult an attorney and financial advisor.

This is your personal choice, and when you make the decision one way or the other, ask your family and friends to support you in your decision. You need love and support now, more than ever.

There are many bereaved parents who have to face difficult and arduous criminal trials if their child was killed. My heart breaks for those of you who have to endure it. Please surround yourself with support and caring people.

There's a saying "if you have fear, you can't have faith." I'm not sure a grieving parent will believe that right now. Faith is the only thing I could cling to, in order to get up every morning, and yet fear was always grabbing at my feet.

"Fear is manufactured in your own mind." —**Joan Z. Borysenko, Ph.D,** author **It's Not the End of the World, Developing Resilience in Times of Change**

When you are grieving the loss of a child, your brain is not functioning like it normally would. You can have the strongest faith in the world, but there's nothing that would make you feel at peace with death at the beginning stages of your grief.

At least that's how I felt.

My fear extended into my family. I realized this when, one day my daughter came to me and said, "Mommy, How do I make the fear in my heart go away?"

I was relieved to begin releasing my fear when I was able to share my thoughts and feelings with my therapist. We worked through it, and eventually I let go of the rituals and the constant obsessive behavior.

"Therefore I tell you, do not worry about your life . . . Who of you by worrying can add a single hour to his life?"—**The Bible,** Matthew 6:27

I learned to replace fear by focusing on loving myself. I found productive things I could do that would have more appropriate time limits than being up all night organizing my library.

I joined a pottery studio and began painting beautiful bowls, plates, and dishes. It got me out of the house and it was an interlude from the obsession of organizing my home.

Then, I began to include my children after school. We'd spend afternoons in the studio, at a table together, painting, talking, and just finding peace in creative expression.

Today, my children tell me those afternoons meant so much to them. They called it "soothing." It also ignited Trevor's passion for art.

This is what Joan Borysenko, author of **Minding the Body, Mending the Mind** calls "stress hardiness." Yes, you've had a horrible tragedy. Optimism and positive thinking doesn't work here. What does work is finding new ways to transition the stress into more manageable activities and time slots.

If you are feeling fear, try not to be too hard on yourself, but acknowledge it to yourself and to others.

Talk about it, seek help if necessary, but get it out in the open so you do not feel "shame" along with grief. It's hard to judge your own sanity because you are in the midst of a grief storm.

Stepping Stones: Acknowledging Fear and Obsessive Behavior

Your behaviors and observations have likely been altered by your loss. Sometimes we can handle it ourselves, and sometimes we need professional help.

I urge you to find a therapist during your grieving process as a safe place to heal and reveal your thoughts without being judged. If your insurance doesn't support therapy, and it's financially difficult to make the commitment, ask your doctor or friend to help you find a free support group in your community.

- **Write down in your journal any new behaviors and rituals you've started since your child died.** Be completely honest and open.
- **Choose someone you trust to tell about those behaviors.** Ask them to help you decide which behaviors are destructive and which are productive. If they are interrupting your quality of life (like taking away from sleep or giving your body a jolt of adrenalin), then they

are destructive. For example, organizing my books in the middle of the night was not really an appropriate choice. It left me exhausted. However, tending my garden during the daytime was productive.

- **Recognize fear and obsessive behavior as a stage of grief** that will usually pass in most cases. Getting help during this time will aid in quicker recovery.

- **Try redirecting obsessive behaviors by implementing new tasks that have time limits** and will get you out of the house to be with people.

- **Meditation is an avenue you can use to help quiet your fearful mind.** At first I could only find tears when I prayed or meditated. I started with just a minute or two, and then worked up to 10 minutes, then 20. Meditative music helps. Just try it, and stay committed.

- **Acknowledge feelings of resentment.** It's a natural part of bereavement, but those feelings can ignite anger and retaliation. Seek help in discussing these feelings.

- **Ask for advice from an attorney or financial advisor if you are considering a lawsuit.** Also discuss the emotional ramifications with your therapist or a trusted advisor.

- **Absolutely seek professional help if your behaviors are harmful** (such as too much drinking, drugs, food addictions, or self destructive behavior). Ask your closest friend or someone you implicitly trust to help guide you and hold you accountable for getting the right help.

Marriage, Relationships, and Grieving

*"Grief can't be shared. Everyone carries it
alone, his own burden, his own way."*
—**Ann Morrow Lindbergh**, author of **Dearly Beloved**

**The most challenged relationship surrounding the death of a
child is the union of two people that created that child.**

I know, because *mine* was. On the outside, my husband and I
appeared to be handling the loss with dignity and grace, but inside
we were pulling apart. What was dying was our ability to love
each other through the shroud of the death of our beloved child.

Struggling through the grief process is hard enough as an
individual, but when you have to make room for the feelings of
your partner, it's overwhelming. When David and I once enjoyed

memories and stories of our history together, now, our history held our greatest tragedy.

We mourned together, but more often we mourned separately. The divisiveness can be damaging and could eventually cause resentment if you don't address it now.

For example, when David would come home from work happy, and it was in stark contrast to my day of feeling Garrett's loss, I resented him. In turn, he resented me for putting a damper on his good day.

It happened the other way too. If I was happy, and he wanted to grieve, a wall went up between us, where no love or connection could tear down the heavy stones of sadness.

It's impossible to give comfort when you are in the depths of despair. You find yourself angry when your partner is happy, or sad, and it's the opposite of how you're feeling. I was given more support from friends and family because women typically reach out more than men.

My husband went back to work within a week. I heard from many who offered my husband comfort. He responded by saying "Oh well, thanks, I'm fine. Those things happen."

He was not fine. He wanted so much to be brave and hold the financial stability of the family together. He also wanted to avoid the inevitable, acknowledging the pain of his broken heart caused by the tragic loss of his firstborn son.

On the outside, he wore an emotional straight jacket, inside; he had a wound that couldn't heal. He did not come out of the darkness for a long time. Instead he found ways to avoid grieving.

This can be destructive for both of you. It's important to realize *you*, as a couple, are at the very core of the family. The two of you are a partnership in holding the family together. If you have other children, they need your united strength.

You may feel a sense of doom in your relationship, like nothing can ever go right again. It clouds everything and you are just waiting for the next thing to happen. This is natural. We feel at our most vulnerable as parents who have lost children.

It's important that you come together in the most loving, compassionate embrace of commitment. You must be committed to each other and just as committed to healing independently.

We were the architects of our child's world, and that world came tumbling down. Those feelings of vulnerability are often difficult to discuss with your partner. This is why it's important to have a professional or a trusted friend to talk to.

"Blaming" can also be a natural part of grieving your loss. It's your attempt to find reason and make sense of your child's death. This is part of the "bargaining phase" of the Five Stages of Grief. In reality, *there is* no way to make sense of a tragic young death.

If you find yourself blaming your partner, however, you will need to seek professional help immediately. It's nearly impossible to weather that storm without a therapist, a counselor, or a group who understands the grieving process.

Don't always expect your partner to comfort you. They can barely comfort themselves. A neutral third party is the perfect approach to feeling safe in discussing grief issues. Seek the help of friends, family, professional counselors, and groups such as

Compassionate Friends (see Stepping Stones at the end of this chapter).

Couples may separately seek solace in co-workers or friends. Be wary of relationships that grow beyond the boundaries of friendship and lead to the possibility of infidelity. It might feel like an escape from the darkness and make one feel temporarily happy, but it can add a whole new dimension to grief. It's called guilt. At this point it's time for professional help.

Some, who have lost a child, say they feel like they've fallen out of love in their marriage.

The truth is, you haven't fallen out of love, it's just that grief is the predominant emotion you are dealing with, and it's hard to focus on refueling your love for each other.

How was your relationship before your child died? If it was strong, loving, and close, then it can be all those things again. But it takes time and attention, and sometimes, professional help. If your relationship struggled before the death of your child, then immediately seek help in counseling.

Once some time has passed, begin thinking about taking time for physical love. Physical closeness can be a challenge. As much as sex may be the last thing on your mind, it's actually a gift you can give yourself, your partner, and your marriage.

Sometimes it may feel like trying to jump start a dead battery, but with nurturing, you can find it brings the greatest reward. It also releases "feel good hormones" which will give your spirit a boost. It's so important to take care of your physical needs right now, and sex is one of them.

Lets go through a few of the stepping stones and discover ways of finding the glue that will keep your relationship together, supportive, and loving. If it appears that resentment, separation, and blame have arisen from the depths of your grief, it's time to seek counseling from a licensed therapist who specializes in grieving parents.

I cannot undervalue the role my therapist played in my healing. She guided me through the grief process, and as a trained professional, helped in ways friends and families couldn't.

Remember, this man (or woman) is your beloved partner in life. You've lost your beautiful child. Don't let the marriage die, too. Feed your relationship with the most love you can possibly express. Your reward is a relationship made stronger when you thought all was lost.

Stepping Stones: Recovering Intimacy and Connection for Couples

"Darling, I am here for you."
"When you love someone, the best thing you can offer is your presence. How can you love if you are not there?"
—**Thich Nhat Hanh,** Zen Buddhist monk, teacher, author

This "couple's exercise" is one you should do shortly after your loss as a specific step in building strength in your relationship. Communicating with your partner and knowing how he or she is coping and being supported is a critical part of grief management and recovery.

- **Share how you feel.** Sit down with each other in a relaxed environment and begin opening up about how you are feeling. If this is difficult to do, seek the help of a licensed therapist to monitor your discussion.
- **Discuss your current support systems and look to your Lifeline List for help.** Identify people you both know and trust who can offer you emotional support during this time. This is not a time for secrets.
- **Develop and maintain healthy friendship/confidant relationships.** It's critically important to choose people you trust (preferably same sex). It's especially critical to be conscious of how you develop and accept support, so you don't find yourself escaping into outside relationships or unhealthy habits.
- **These trusted people will be your emotional support** because it is often too difficult for your mate to handle your grief as well as his own.
- **Recognize that resentment can arise when your partner is feeling happy and you are feeling sad, or vice versa.** This is normal and the reason why we sometimes need to vent our emotions outside of our relationship.

Stepping Stones: Scheduling Time Together

Your schedules will become a critical part of your recovery process.

- **Schedule quality time with your partner.** Consider a dinner date, or a quiet dinner at home after the children have gone to bed. Plan something quiet and relaxing in advance, so you are sure to use this time productively.
- **Prepare yourself emotionally for the night out.** This is not a time to be sad. You may feel sad, but sadness is also a decision you can control. Think of the times when you may have felt sad, but something funny struck you, and you laughed. That's just how sadness can be controlled.
- **Before you're alone with your partner, take a moment to reflect** and consider your partner's feelings, point of view, and daily experiences. This prepares you with empathy and allows you to be more open and conscious of his or her reactions and needs.

Stepping Stones: Anger Issues

- **Anger is a normal step in the 5 stages of grief.**
- **Anger can be destructive** when taken out on your partner or children.
- **Learn to diffuse anger** by recognizing it as a stage of grief and apologizing quickly.

- **Learn to take deep breaths and stop yourself** from verbally or physically harming another person.
- **Unexpressed anger can cause as many problems as expressed anger.** If you have angry feelings, recognize them and discuss with a trusted friend or therapist.
- **Recognize when your feelings of anger are out of control and seek professional help immediately.**

GRIEF AND YOUR WORKPLACE

"Every challenge in your life demands a different you."
-Bob Donnell, Coach, **Next Level 4 Success**
and a father who lost a daughter

At this stage of your loss, you're wondering how in the world you can even find enough strength to focus on work. Grieving monopolizes every single thought and action. Functioning at even the simplest level can be difficult. We struggle to find a way for our work to mean something in the midst of this grief storm.

The key to getting back to work is planning . . . and baby steps. If you work for yourself, you have more flexibility. If you work for someone else, it's imperative you speak with your supervisor or manager to construct the best way to return to work.

At the time of Garrett's death, my husband was producing and writing a television series called **Silk Stalkings**. The show was a weekly series, so David's job was fast paced, intense, and highly demanding.

David went back to work after only a week. He struggled. There were days he became frustrated and found it difficult to write.

He quickly got to the "anger" stage of grief in the stress of trying to function. He wanted to instantly feel better by returning to routine, but life was no longer routine, because he had lost his son. The fog of grief dominated his brain.

Working is a necessary part of maintaining the quality of our lives, but *really* difficult during this time.

Everyone's coping mechanisms—especially with the loss of a child—are different, and its not uncommon to want to stay busy with day-to-day tasks to help handle the shock and grief.

In the long run, your mental and physical health will be critical to helping you work through these challenges, so taking care of yourself is key. An important part of this is evaluating your day-to-day day responsibilities at work. Consider taking some time off and/or reducing some of your workload.

Discuss the timing of returning to work with your partner or advisor. Assess your finances and what impact it will have if you take time off.

It's important to have stability in your job. Going back to work too early can compromise your efficiency and effectiveness in the workplace. If you're in a high—pressure job where lives depend on your attention, it can be dangerous.

If the death of your child also caused mounting medical bills, you may be facing overwhelming financial burden. This is a time to talk with a financial advisor.

Please, do not make any major decisions such as selling your home, changing jobs, or moving away at this time. You need time to analyze how this loss will impact the rest of your life.

You're already having to make one major adjustment in your life: living *without* your beautiful child. Please do not compound the adjustment by adding more changes to your life. If your reasoning is financial, get advice from someone you trust.

Please don't think you can figure this out by yourself. This is a time to turn it over to experts.

Ask your circle of friends whom they recommend to help you. Your church or community services may be able to point you in the right direction, as well.

Most importantly, you may be feeling ineffective at work, unable to concentrate, and as though work doesn't matter anymore. This is a phase you are going through. Know that with the right support and care of your bereavement, your capabilities, focus, and enthusiasm for what you do, will return.

Stepping Stones: Assess Your Responsibilities and Workload

- **Begin by listing in your workbook, all areas in your life in which you have key responsibilities.** Think about major categories such as career, household, and children.
- **Review each area separately and circle the responsibilities** that you feel you *must* continue to fulfill over the next few months. For example, if your career

requires a project for a client with a specific timeline you might have to complete this, but you may be able to postpone or decline extra work or projects.

- **Assess your financial responsibilities** and make a decision as to how much time you can afford to take off, if necessary.

- **If you have mounting bills and feel overwhelmed, consult a financial advisor for help.** Medical bills can also put a tremendous financial and emotional burden on you. Ask for guidance.

- **If you are in a dangerous or high profile job** where lives depend on your attention, consider getting a professional evaluation from a therapist before returning to work.

- **List responsibilities that can be delegated out** for at least several weeks.

- **Sit down with someone from your Lifeline List and make a plan** for how people can organize to help you complete basic tasks that you find difficult to do right now. These can be tasks as simple as carpooling children, taking a vehicle for repair, grocery shopping, laundry, or cooking. Have someone help you reach out to others and engage them in supporting you with these tasks.

- **Remember that others will want to help and offer practical support**, especially in the first few months after your loss because it's a natural way for them to communicate their own feelings of grief.

YOUR LIVING CHILDREN
ARE CRYING TOO

"Many times in our society children are the forgotten grievers."
—**David Kessler**, Author of **Visions,
Trips, and Crowded Rooms**

How in the world do you take care of your living children when your life is consumed with the one who died? This is a question we, as parents who have lost children, ask every morning when we awaken to the tragedy.

This is one of the most difficult challenges, but it's one that cannot be ignored. While you're experiencing the loss of your child, they are experiencing the loss of their brother or sister, *and* they feel like they're losing their parents to grief. It frightens them.

Within hours after my son died, our home was suddenly filled with friends and family bringing food, love, and attention. Even though I was in shock, I felt a certain sense of needing to entertain, as odd as that seems. I made a point of talking to everyone and thanking them for coming, arranging food on the table, and pouring drinks.

But where were my children?

Looking back, I remember my 12-year old son, Trevor, retreated to his room. Our friend, Bruce Boxleitner, went back to Trevor's bedroom and found him there . . . alone, frightened, and sad. He stayed with him in the bedroom for hours.

On that terrible day, I don't remember if I gave my children the attention they needed from me. I'm sure they felt somewhat emotionally abandoned, because I can hardly recall even discussing what happened to their brother. I must have, but everything is such a fog.

My young children couldn't possibly comprehend what had just happened. They just knew they felt sadness, fear, and confusion. They didn't really know what it meant, "to die."

In the past, we had several small pet funerals like for fish and lizards. We created crosses with twigs and lay stones where their beloved pet was buried. We even held a ceremony, saying a few words about how we would miss them and hoped they would go to pet heaven.

But this was different. It was incomprehensible. Somehow their brother went to sleep the night before and never woke up. His body was swiftly taken away in an ambulance. They couldn't even say goodbye.

And unexpectedly, our home was filled with people expressing raw emotion, unfiltered tears, and the focus was entirely on their brother Garrett, who suddenly disappeared.

When you're in shock and subsequently grief, your brain becomes a fog. It's a protection and a cushion. Often, you don't make the right decisions or even have conversations that make sense.

Perhaps my children would rather have been alone with my husband and me instead of being in a house full of people in sorrow in the days following Garrett's death. Perhaps they would have felt safer in our arms, consoling each other.

But often, that's not how it works in our culture.

A few days later, my children would begin to reveal signs of despair.

"I know I miss Garrett, Mommy, because I wake up with tears in my eyes." That was how Julianne described the loss of her brother. She let me know with a look or an embrace, or even tears.

She would often share her dreams with me. She would say, "I know where Garrett is . . . he told me." Pointing up to the sky. Or, "I dream about Garrett every night, but I just can't remember."

Trevor, just 12 years old at the time, retreated. I would reach for him, and he would pull away. He spent so much time in his room and never wanted to talk. Every reply was just a single word. He would spend hours drawing on scraps of paper and painting on his closet wall.

Trevor's anger was palpable. There was a wall no one could break through, although we tried with therapy, school counselors, youth pastors, but nothing could heal his wounds. He pulled away from the family. He felt angry, alone, and guilty.

Why guilt? This can be a typical reaction. Siblings often question, "Would my parents rather have had *me* be the one

to die?" It's important to reassure them that you are so grateful they are alive and with you. Tell them how much you love them. Hold them, kiss them, and express your love to them now, more than you ever have.

Trevor internalized his sadness and looked for ways not to feel anything. He revealed to me years later, kids approached him at school right after Garrett died and offered him drugs. They said it would help him feel better. He asked me to include this extremely personal information in this book, in hopes that it might save other children.

Jackson was the reason I had to get out of bed in the morning because he was just a year old and still nursing. In the early morning hours, we would lie on the couch and watch "Sesame Street." He would giggle and laugh.

Jackson also felt the sorrow. There was no sadness revealed in his face because he still had his child's heart where everything is amazing, entertaining, and enchanting. But, he would suddenly pet my face and say "Mommy sad?"

He took on the roll of "the comforter." For some, this could have been a huge problem in growing up.

The need to please is one that children often adopt when they see their parents in pain. It can create a lifelong struggle with co-dependency.

In later years, he became a child that was eternally happy and ready to give love. It wasn't until Jackson's teen years, that he began to feel the loss of a brother he never really knew. We tried to heal the hole as much as we could with stories of Garrett, photos, and family videos.

As a parent you have a unique and complex role of both grieving your lost child and supporting and parenting your surviving children.

Julianne was just five when Garrett died. Instead of showing tears, she turned to laughter. She became a child that always seemed happy, but struggled with sadness inside. I never felt compelled to dwell on whether she was okay, because she always seemed okay.

But she wasn't. She was so very sad, and she didn't know how to cry her tears without upsetting her mom and dad. I wish she had. Then, I would have known.

At the age of 22 she was brave enough to ask me if she could start therapy. Therapy has helped heal her heart, as well as our communication.

Trevor was so deeply wounded. Ultimately, he found his outlet through art. He could have remained in the cocoon of grief, but he worked through it.

Some children act out, some may be vulnerable to drugs, and really anything that might make them feel better. They don't have adult emotions and reasoning yet, so they do whatever feels good. **Grieving for siblings is very similar as it is for parents losing a child, but recognize that each child handles it differently.** Be consistent in talking with your children about their feelings.

Just as you will need a circle of support, it's also critical to ensure that your surviving children are spending time with supportive adults and friends who *they* feel comfortable and safe with.

Reassure your children that they *are* safe.

In the early weeks, they may want to sleep in your room with you. My children slept in sleeping bags beside our bed for a few weeks. It made them feel safe.

Constantly reinforce your love for them. Allow each of them to have "alone" time with you. All the daily love you demonstrated to your child who died, now needs to be tucked away (not gone) and redirected to your living children.

Above all, give them the gift of healing *yourself* so they feel they haven't lost their mommy and daddy to grief.

Stepping Stones: Guidance for Siblings

As parents it's important to stay in tune and frequently check in with your surviving children's emotions. Ask questions and really listen to how they are doing.

- **Ask your children open-ended questions** rather than "yes and no" questions. This leaves room for their thoughts.
- **Open-ended questions begin with *what, how, who, and why*.** For example, "How did your dream about your brother make you feel?" What did the two of you do?" or "What colors were in your dream?" If the colors were

bright, how did they make him feel, if they were dark, how did they make him feel?

- **Try not to answer or guide your child's answers.** For example, don't say, "Did the dark colors in your dream make you feel afraid?" That tells him he should feel fear. You don't want to influence that feeling if he didn't come up with the idea himself. If *he* says it made him feel afraid, then you can explore further . . . why, how, etc.

- **Avoid closed ended questions** that begin with *Do, Did you, When, Do you want to, Will you,* and *Have you.* All they require is a "yes'" or a "no."

Write down your observations in your workbook/journal about each child's behavior and patterns. It will help you stay aware of any changes in their behavior. Consider how to best support each child's individual style of grieving.

- **Who are the adults that your child or children feel safest with? Consider asking your child.** It can be either family members or friends. Write these names in your journal. Ultimately, you can decide who is the best person to help.

- **Make an appointment with your child's school counselor** *before* they go back to school. Explain what happened and ask for their help. Often, schools have programs for children dealing with grief. I have worked with the school system here, in conducting a grief group for children who have lost family members. It's amazing to see the growth from the first week of the course to the eighth week. Not only are they stronger and happier, they have also formed lifelong friendships with others in the group.

- **Describe each child's behavior in your journal.** Are they growing quiet, spending a lot of time alone, or are they trying to be more active and engaged as part of coping?

- **Do you notice changes in specific daily habits** such as appetite, sleep schedule, and overall mood? Sadness and difficulties are something you can expect, but if you notice any extreme changes such as serious nightmares, lack of eating, or prolonged crying spells you should consult a doctor or counselor for some professional input.

- **Does your child seem to want to talk about his or her sibling?** Is counseling something he or she would feel comfortable with or supported by? Some children want to talk, while others are simply not as comfortable.

- **What is making your child feel better right now?** (sports, music, art, etc.). Implement activities that make them feel good.

- **Is there anything that is making the situation more difficult** for him or her and are there ways that you and your partner can provide cushioning and support.

- **Watch for negative influences.** Shortly after Garrett died, Trevor was approached by kids at school who had drugs. They told him drugs would make him feel better.

Monitor whether your child is suddenly hanging around with a different group of friends.

- **Watch their schoolwork.** How are their grades? Are they participating responsibly in their activities? Are they doing their homework when they should? Contact their school counselor with concerns.

- **Be careful not to hover, or restrict their childhood.** For example, one parent whose child died in a pool accident restricted her other children from swimming. This causes resentment and fear in your living children.

- **Spend time each morning or evening to sit together** with each child alone, and play or talk. Continually reassure them of your love and presence.

- **Always plan a family meal together.** Years down the road, when I asked my children what helped them the most . . . they said it was the family dinner because they knew we would all be together and it also held them accountable for good behavior (not getting into trouble after school!).

- **Check the bibliography for children and teens** for suggested reading that you and your children can do together to help process this loss. The list is on my website: www.SandyPeckinpah.com

Stepping Stones: Pets

Bereavement is a time when pets can bring a great deal of comfort for children and adults. I wouldn't necessarily encourage getting a new pet, because it's hard to train a new animal when emotions are raw and attention is scattered. It is the perfect time, however, to connect with your pet as a source of comfort for you and your children.

- **Because your pet's** nature is to be unconditional love, they want to please you. At this time they can be great comfort to you and your children.
- **Encourage neighborhood walks with your dog.** Hopefully, you'll have an opportunity to see compassionate neighbors along the way.
- **Give your cat extra "lap" time.**
- **Schedule time with your children for taking care of your pets** such as baths, brushing, training, playing ball.
- **Take a "nature day" and go hiking with your pet.** Pack a lunch, water for you and your pet, and a leash. Always take a cell phone in case you lose your way.

THE MYSTICAL MAGICAL CHILD IN HEAVEN

Cultivate a resilient life by cultivating a resilient spirit

Often siblings, and sometimes parents will re-invent history.
You will find them telling stories you don't remember. Their
recollections are colored by the way they feel. They might even
disagree with each other in how the story actually happened.

They make up ways they could have changed the death of
their sibling. This is *bargaining*, a stage of grief. They are thinking
if they had done something differently, it never would have
happened.

I did it myself when I thought *if only I awakened an hour
earlier, instead of oversleeping, I could have revived him.* The truth
is, my son's meningitis was so virulent throughout his body, even
the doctor couldn't have saved him. It took me years before I made
peace with the truth. I re-framed my feelings and began to find

serenity in knowing the last thing I said to him was "I love you" and kissed him goodnight.

Your children may feel especially vulnerable, as though something bad could happen to them. Try to reassure them of your love and protection. Help them feel safe by listening and answering their questions and concerns.

Children will ask questions like "Where did he go when he died?" They might ask, "But you said we lost him, why can't you find him?" "Where is heaven?"

One day, Melissa and I took our children to the cemetery to place flowers at Garrett's grave. This was the first time Melissa's five-year old son, Dakota, had been to the cemetery. He'd heard us say, "We're going to take flowers to Garrett." When we arrived, he hopped out of the car and ran across the grass with Julianne and Jackson. Julianne stopped at Garrett's headstone. "Here he is!" she exclaimed.

There was a tube buried in the ground at the base of the headstone where the flowers would sit. Dakota, dropped to his knees, put his mouth to the tube and yelled into it, "Garrett! You can come out now!"

And yes . . . Melissa and I laughed uncontrollably (and it felt good). We realized that Dakota had no conception of what it meant when he was told that Garrett died.

Explore your child's understanding of death and heaven. Help guide them to a spiritual belief that brings comfort.

I found my church and Sunday School to be a great resource. Others may find comfort in other religions and beliefs. Whatever those beliefs might be, hold onto them for strength.

Your children need to believe in something right now and so do you. I don't care how mad you are with God, or whatever you believe in, it's critical to your children to help them find faith and comfort. It's the only thing that will carry them through life after this tragic, tragic event.

We will do exercises that help you and your children identify, develop, and find faith and comfort in their beliefs.

I've mentioned in a previous chapter, the importance of having dinner together. I can't stress this enough. Offer it as a time to talk. If you can't find the energy to prepare meals, ask for help. Look to your **Lifeline List** in your journal for friends who can organize dinners for you for the first month.

At the dinner table, let the children guide the conversation where they want it to go. Ask them questions about school, friends, play, and anything that interests them. Make sure all cell phones, televisions, iPads, and computers are off and away from the table. This is your time to focus on your family.

Your children may want to relate stories about their missing sibling, or they may not. Pick some interesting current topics to bring into the conversation at the dinner table. This is the time to learn to be a family in a new way.

You are *always* going to wish your child was a part of your future life events. However, be aware that when you say, "I wish he was here," then your living children may have the feeling that something is missing, and true happiness is impossible.

If you make the story you tell about your child one that is impossible for your other children to live up to, it can damage their self-esteem for a lifetime.

Stepping Stones: The True Story

- **Let your child (or children) talk about their brother or sister however they choose.** Tell stories often and use them as a way to let them vent their emotion, whether it's laughter or tears.
- **Help your children identify, develop, and find faith and comfort in their beliefs.** The best person to help you with this is your pastor. If you don't belong to a church, turn to your **Lifeline List** for a friend who has faith. Ask for guidance and resource recommendations to help your children understand the concept of what happens when someone dies. Like Dakota, they might not have any conception of what happens when someone dies.
- **Be careful in how you deify your child.** Like all people, there are good qualities and bad qualities, but you don't want to make your child who died impossible for his brothers and sisters to live up to.
- **Every time you have a milestone in the years ahead,** if you say, "Oh, I wish he was here to see this," then your living children will grow up to feel that there is always something missing. What a horrible burden to feel nothing is ever going to be good enough.
- **Sometimes a sibling may think *they* should have been the one to die.** They can experience tremendous guilt. They may question in their minds, *would Mom and Dad be happier if it had been me that died?* Reinforce your love for them. They need to hear it now more than ever.

- **It's important you maintain family stability by adhering to your daily patterns**. One young boy I counseled after the death of his brother said he really missed family dinners. Structure is important at this time.

If you question their healing process or feel their behavior is destructive, you need to immediately get your child professional help. Ask your school counselors for recommendations.

The Pearly Gates . . .
Believing In Miracles

Yes, They Happen

*"Sometimes the answer to a prayer is not that
it changes life, but that it changes you."*
-James Dillet Freeman, Author of **"BE!"**
and Poet Laureate to the moon

I was raised in the Presbyterian Church, and yet I am not sure what I really believed about heaven. I never had to know. I know for sure, I believed if I was a good girl, nothing bad would ever happen.

I was very young when I formed my vision of Heaven. It was the great unknown city above the clouds where God lived. My Grandma told me God greeted all the people who die at the Pearly Gates of Heaven. And, my Grandma's name was Pearl, so I thought she must have been someone really special. Then she died, and I felt like there was so much more I needed to know and could never ask her. Like, how she made her applesauce and why did she want me to read the Bible. I pictured her arriving at the Pearly Gates and everyone would know her because she was Pearl.

When my son died, the beautiful image of the Pearly Gates didn't matter because all of my beliefs were thrown into chaos. I asked, "How can I know if there's a God? Where is heaven? Is there really an afterlife? Is my Grandma there?

These are all questions we, as intelligent adults may have at different times in our lives, but never is it more profound than now . . . when *your* child is missing from this earth.

Was I angry with God? You bet. How could *He* have allowed this to happen to *me*? I did everything right and yet I lost a child! A child! How could that have happened to such a "good girl?"

The truth is, why not me? Others have lost children and they were "good girls" too.

I realized my perceived belief system collided with real human experience.

We are not human beings having a spiritual experience. We are spiritual beings having a human experience.—**Pierre Teilhard de Chardin**, French Philosopher and Jesuit Priest

My only choice was to re-examine my faith.

Step One: Did I believe in God? Yes.

Step Two: Was I open to the possibility that God exists and has a plan for my life? Yes.

Step Three: Was I willing to acknowledge that sometimes the human experience involves getting sick, sometimes dying, or having a tragic accident? Yes, reluctantly.

Step Four: Am I able to survive such tragic loss? Yes, yes, and yes, because at this point in my life, it's not about me, I would just as soon die than feel this pain. But this is about love. Love for my husband and my living children.

And so . . . I chose to be open to and believe in the possibility that there really is something above those clouds called heaven. A place where my beautiful boy crossed through the Pearly Gates and met his Grandma Pearl for the very first time and felt the comfort of her soft squishy embrace.

C.S Lewis (1898-1963), an author and arguably the most influential Christian writer of his day, wrote a book about his sorrow when he lost his wife. It's titled **A Grief Observed**, and was subsequently made into a movie called **Shadowlands**. His ruminations questioning his faith and belief in God resonated with me. Here was a man who spent his life writing about faith, and yet even *he* questioned his beliefs when his beloved wife died.

Faith is all we have right now. When you lose your child, you absolutely have to implement faith as your lifeline. You can't do this alone. I know you question God and Heaven and Creation right now, but if you believe in nothing you are lost. You will never heal.

The "knowing" that there is a God, goes beyond intellect. Look at yourself. Look at the miracle that was created by you, inside of you. You created a child. Is that a miracle explained simply by chance?

Sometimes we think . . . give me a sign. But isn't your child being born, sign enough that there is something much greater than we can ever fathom?

Science can tell you the story of how it happened, but how does it happen that the body is formed from one chance moment in time, where tiny cells meet and become human. Those little cells joyfully joined together and gave you a child. And that is a miracle.

Just as you know someone is in the next room even though he is not with you; God is present, even though you cannot see him, and *so is your child*. Your spirit and your child's spirit are energy, and energy never dies.

Build faith by opening your mind and your heart to miracles. You may have them in the form of dreams, nature, even a song on the radio. These are postcards from your child.

Anniversaries, Birthdays, and Holidays often accentuate loss. These are times when families typically gather together and have rituals attached. When your child is missing from these upcoming events, it can be really heart wrenching.

My son died December 19th, 6 days before Christmas. For years, following his death, I began to anticipate the emptiness as the holidays approached. I would awaken with dread, and fall asleep to it. I realized that often, the anticipation was actually worse than the actual day.

As a family, we had to create new rituals and incorporate memories of Garrett within it. On Christmas Eve, I still hang his stocking by the fireplace. We still make a ritual of placing his baby ornament on the tree. We read his favorite Christmas Story, **A Christmas Memory** by Truman Capote. And we always include him in our prayers at the dinner table.

Inevitably there is always a miracle arriving around the time of holidays or anniversaries. It's sometimes as simple as a rainbow or a bird singing at my window.

On the Friday before my first Mother's Day without my child, my heart was heavy with grief. I picked up the children from school and headed to Gelson's for groceries. I wanted to prepare a dinner that would involve a lot of "doing" in order to numb myself from the pain. I decided on Fresh Vegetable Pasta. It involved lots of chopping, grilling and sautéing.

As we perused the grocery aisles, the kids were throwing things into the basket, and I was blind to it. One bag of groceries turned into six, but I didn't care.

A young man (who was a friend of my son) carefully bagged the groceries, and offered to take them out to the car. As we walked, I asked him about his college plans. As he closed the trunk, I slipped him a tip and thanked him. I watched him walk away with his dreams intact. He was alive. His parents could watch him become a man.

I was embarrassed to feel such awe followed by anger.

"I have to make a stop, before we go home." The children heard my voice tremble, and it made them quiet during the ride.

I pulled into the cemetery at dusk. I slowly drove the familiar road through the grounds. I noticed lots of new flowers at some of the plots. *Must be for all the Moms,* I thought.

I parked.

"Why don't you start your homework in the car? I'll be right back. I opened the trunk and pulled out the basket, fully stocked at all times with paper towels, marble cleaner, a scrubbing brush, plant shears, and a spray bottle of water.

It was a familiar ritual I'd begun as soon as Garrett was buried. I was robbed of the years ahead tending to folding his clothes, straightening his room, and picking up dirty socks. I transferred my duties to keeping his gravesite impeccable.

Every day, I brought my basket to snip, scrub, and clean his "new room." It gave me time to talk to him, alone, and to care for him.

As I approached the grave, I could feel my teary eyes stinging against the cool night breeze. I threw my basket down and fell to my knees in front of Garrett's stone and began to cry.

"Mother's Day is coming Garrett, and you're not here, dammit! I'm *so* angry with you for leaving me! I don't know how to do this."

I tried to keep my body straight so the children wouldn't see how distraught I was. But sometimes I was just exhausted from having to be so strong.

I sprayed water onto the stone and used the brush to scrub the letters of his name. I wiped it clean, then polished. The strands of grass were still neat and tidy from yesterday's visit.

"Please Garrett, please let me know you're with me. I gave life to you! Tell me, you're here, tell me . . ." I cried, hoping for a magical response. I waited, none came.

I shifted to see the children watching me from the car. *Call to duty. Straighten up. Be your best for them.* I packed up my tools.

I kissed my fingers and touched his stone, stood up and walked back stoically.

We got home to a dark house. I flicked on the kitchen lights and saw the message button flashing on the answering machine. I pushed it. David's voice played, "Hi Sandy, I'm gonna be a little late tonight. Go ahead and feed the kids. Love you."

Damn, a nice family dinner was supposed to heal the wounds of today. I abandoned my plans for the pasta and decided on tacos. I had everything left over from the night before.

Trevor came into the kitchen, "I'm hungry, now."

"I'm fixing dinner as fast as I can, sweetie."

"But I'm hungry, now. Can't I just have a popsicle?"

"No Trevor, I'm fixing tacos."

"Tacos? He protested, "We had those last night."

Julianne came bounding in. I sat Jackson in the high chair and handed him a fistful of dry cereal. Patience.

"I have a good idea. Both of you. Go clean your rooms! Now! They're a mess! When you're done, dinner will be ready."

They retreated meekly to their rooms.

Sandy . . . Patience. I began to pull out everything for tacos. I poured oil into a frying pan and waited for it to sizzle.

Silly. I could have bought the pre-made crispy tacos. They wouldn't have cared. Garrett would have, though. He was always my picky eater. Garrett . . . Mother's Day . . . empty . . . . my thoughts began to spiral out of control.

"Mom . . . . Mom . . ." I lifted myself from the daze to see Trevor beside me. He was clutching a hand made card. I looked at him and touched his face. "I'm sorry, honey, I'm just really missing your brother right now."

"Mom . . ." holding the card, his hand began to tremble. "I found this stuck behind the desk drawer when I was cleaning it out."

Trevor had asked for Garrett's old desk. We moved it into Trevor's room a few days before.

I took the card from his hand. It was *Garrett's* handwriting.

"What is this, honey?" I asked. I began to read it aloud.

"Mom! Happy Mother's Day!"

I looked at Trevor, dumbfounded. I opened the card Garrett had written and read:

Mom, you are a very special person-you really are.
Who else could write 2 books and raise 4 kids at the same time?!
A big heart is needed to do both of those things,
And a big heart is what you have.
Happy Mother's Day, Mom
I love you very much,
Love, Garrett

Trevor said in disbelief, "He must have written it before he died, Mom."

"But he died at Christmas!" I said in awe.

A feeling of peace filled all those empty places in my soul. *Garrett heard me, he's truly here,* I thought.

"Trevor, thank you for finding this, you've given me a wonderful gift." Trevor smiled so sweetly. I hugged him close.

"I love your tacos, Mom," he said sheepishly.

Julianne joined in. "Me too! I could eat them *every* night!"

My husband opened the door . . . Hey family! What's for dinner?"

Tacos!" they all replied.

"Good," David said, "I love tacos."

The grilled vegetable pasta would be just fine for tomorrow.

Look for miracles. They do happen. Invite them into your life. When they happen, be grateful and say a prayer of thanks. Then invite more miracles to arrive.

The question about miracles that I'm frequently asked is: "Has your son visited you or come to you in your dreams?" The answer is "yes."

The first dream was just a few weeks after Garrett died. Many have followed. Some are like dreams, but some are very real and there's an undeniable feeling of their presence. You may even smell the scent of flowers, or some aroma that characterizes their essence.

One night, I even felt the presence of my son sitting down on the edge of the bed. I felt it, but I couldn't see him. I could hear him in my mind, though.

It can happen in a song you hear on the radio "by accident" at the serendipitous moment you were thinking about your child. You feel it and you know it's your child's presence. Sing with that song and know he's singing with you.

Loss gives you a whole new set of beliefs about what's possible. It's not a time to shut down; rather, it's a time to open your heart to the possibility of miracles and to honor them by believing they can happen. Write them down when you experience them so you will never, ever forget.

Miracles are postcards from heaven reassuring you there *is* a place above the clouds where your beloved child entered through the Pearly Gates and wants you to know, it's beautiful there.

Stepping Stones: Building Faith and Recognizing Miracles

"If you lose your expectation, you lose your potential for a miracle."
-**Bishop T.D. Jakes,** Pastor of **The Potter's House Church**

Miracles will begin coming your way when you commit to faith and start to believe they are possible. Miracles come in many forms. Sometimes they are as simple as a dove calling at your window. My daughter believes that every time she finds a dime, it's a message from above.

- **Invite miracles into your life**. When they happen, be grateful and say a prayer of thanks. Then invite more miracles to arrive.
- **In a quiet room, close your eyes and visualize your child**. Tears may fall from your eyes, but that's okay. Those are tears of connection.
- **Now ask your child to give you a gift.**
- **Stay with your child in your mind, and tell them you will be fine.** Tell them tears are not a storm of sadness, but a shower of love.
- **Ask your child to visit in your dreams.**
- **Now say goodbye and open your eyes.**
- **In your workbook/journal, document this day.**
- **Throughout the days ahead, start noticing things like rainbows, stones, birds, and things your child may have loved.**
- **Parents who have walked this path before you will all tell you they experienced miracles in many ways.** Just start recognizing what might be a miracle. Write them down in your journal and you'll begin to see a pattern of gifts from your child.

My son used to pick a single white rose for me on the way home from school. Whenever I see a single white rose, I think *Garrett? Is that you?*

And somehow the rose seems to open out to me and in its beauty says . . . *"I love you, Mom."*

And that is the power of a miracle.

YOUR LIBRARY
OF HEALING

*Within books, I found evidence that others have walked the path
of grief before me and I knew, without a doubt, I would survive.*

You are in emotional upheaval, a fight for your life like you've never
known before. You need knowledge, support, and reinforcement.
One of the places I found solace was in the path of others who've
walked before me.

Our friend, Stephen J. Cannell showed up at our door on the
day that Garrett died. A year before, Stephen had hired David to
be the Executive Producer and writer for a new television series
called **Silk Stalkings**.

Here was a man who was as powerful as they get in the
television world; creating shows like **Rockford Files**, **The A
Team**, and **Hunter**. And yet, tragedy lay beneath his powerful
personae. Stephen and his wife lost their 15-year old child several

years before. We knew about it, everyone who worked with him did, but we never dreamed it could happen to us.

Stephen arrived at our home with a book in his hands, **The Bereaved Parent**. "Sadly, you've joined our club," he said, "parents who've lost children." He handed me the book. I opened it.

The inscription read, *"Dear David and Sandy, Hope you will be able to read this . . . it really helped us. Love, Marcia and Stephen.*

For the next several weeks, I kept that book in my purse and read it every time I doubted my ability to survive. It was my lifeline to *hope*.

David and I were writers. We also loved to read.

We turned to books to find information and support in words. Steve's book to us was the first in our "Library of Healing."

We found peace in words, and faith that if others had gotten through it . . . so could we.

I urge you to go through the **Bibliography of Spiritual, and Mindful Support** on my website (www.SandyPeckinpah.com) and find some publications and books that resonate with you. They will help you along the way, not only with yourself, but also with your children, your family, and your friends.

Not all books are a fit at this time, but they may speak powerfully to you later. Just keep researching.

Books give you guidance, and can help uncover and develop your faith. **No one should ever have to walk through life without faith.** It's the only thing we can really hold onto for resilience.

*"I would go so far as to say that if your God is not a
God of unconditional love, get another God!"*
—**Robert Holden, Ph.D.** author, **Shift Happens**!

Stepping Stones: Library of Healing

It's very important that you honor your loss and the exceptional challenges it is bringing to your life. The loss of a child is a very unique and profound loss for any parent. Reading and learning more about the psychological effects of this loss and the complex recovery process is a key way to actively work on the challenges you face.

You don't have to inundate yourself with materials on loss and grief. You can look for motivational and inspirational books too.

- **Research online or at the library, books on grief.** If you can afford to buy the books, do so. I encourage you to underline and highlight in your books. It helps to be able to pick up a book and quickly see highlighted thoughts that could turn your day around. I kept a book in my purse at all times.
- **Buy inspirational books**, along with books on grief.
- **Read outside the box.** You are developing a new way of living. Take a chance with books that are non-traditional for you.

- **Read books about people you admire who have experienced and overcome tragedies.** It brings to light that virtually everyone on this planet faces tragedies and challenges at some point in life.

- **Read spiritual, inspiring books for at least 15 minutes every morning before getting out of bed.** I read The Bible, and C.S. Lewis books.

- **Consider writing your own story of recovery.** Even if you've never written before, you can tell your own story in your own words. Sometimes seeing it on paper helps heal your heart. If you share it with others, you are giving the gift of your insight to others.

- **There is a bibliography of book recommendations at www.SandyPeckinpah.com, along with suggested websites and music that will help you heal.**

THE RESILIENT ROSE

The Gifts of Nature
*"She who loves a garden learns the lessons of the seasons
and how life itself adheres to nature's plan."*—**Mary
Engelbreit**, author, "**She Who Loves a Garden**"

We often refer to life as a journey or a path. I always pictured my life on a magical pathway winding through trees, leaping on stepping-stones across a babbling brook, the sun brightly shining above a deep blue sky.

In grief, the imagined sky can feel very dark and stormy. The babbling brook is like an impossible, un-crossable raging rapid, and the beautiful trees are a dark shrouded scary forest.

Life reflects nature and nature reflects life.

After my son died, my friend Jody brought me a book, "**She Who Loves a Garden**," by Mary Engelbreit. In this whimsical book, it says, *"She who loves a garden learns the lessons of the seasons and how life itself adheres to nature's plan."*

Jody inscribed the book with this thought,

"My dear friend, Sandy, No one, not even God, will ever take your garden away."

She offered to help me create my garden of healing.

We decided to plant a rose garden. The rose represents resilience. In the winter, roses are cut back to sticks and stripped of leaves. The bushes weather the frost, and somehow manage to bloom every spring, no matter what.

As my garden took shape, my wonderful circle of friends began bringing me roses of every kind. I would open my front door in the morning, and there would be another rose bush, waiting to be planted in what I called "Garrett's Garden."

Children made wind chimes and colorful signs; others brought birdbaths, fountains, and gardening tools for nurturing the garden.

I carefully labeled each plant, documenting who gave it to me, and what day it arrived.

My children often helped me dig, pull weeds and plant. I loved it. It was joyful! I felt connected to Garrett and my living children as we tended the garden.

In this garden, my husband and I established a new relationship with our son. It was a place we could go to share stories, sometimes laughter as we recalled so many wonderful memories.

Through the process over the years, I learned how to get my hands dirty, how to control aphids with lady bugs and a forceful spray of the hose, how to fight the gophers by filling their holes with water, how to keep rabbits away with blood meal, and how to shoo away the graceful deer (who looked to my garden for dessert) with a sound machine (it worked <u>just</u> sometimes).

Ahhh, the cycles of life, I was learning that all forms of life offer challenges and ultimately to accept what I couldn't control. My garden brought me peace and was a place to "ground" myself and bury my sorrow.

Every year was a new beginning. As I cut back the roses in winter, I knew, without a doubt, they would bloom again in the spring. I could hold God and nature responsible for losing my blooms to the deer, the gophers, the rabbits, and the aphids.

Ultimately He would give me an opportunity to start again as tender leaves sprouted from brown rose stumps. As soon as I saw signs of tender green shoots popping through the winter hardened dirt, I knew a glorious garden of color was just a few short weeks away. My garden became one of triumph.

When you sit in your garden, begin to recognize miracles in the gifts of nature. Open your eyes and your heart to all that lies before you. Listen to the bird singing you a song. Listen to the trickling water as a harp for your heart, and allow the sky to hold you in its embrace.

Those are the miracles that taught me life does indeed have good cycles and tragic cycles; and yet from it, rebirth emerges. The challenges and sorrows are just as important as the joys and the glorious blooms in shaping your garden of life.

Resilience lies somewhere, deep inside our souls, ready to spring forth from the roots of tragedy. When we emerge, it opens us to the glory of a life fully lived.

"All of nature is resurrection."
Brian L. Weiss, MD, Author of **Miracles Happen**

Stepping Stones: Using Nature to Heal Life's Challenges

I offer you a new way to traverse the challenges that life gives you by using the lessons of nature to renew your spirit.

- **Consider Planting a Garden.** From your list of friends, find the one friend who has a green thumb. Ask them to help you plant a garden.

- **Watch for the Gifts!** Once you start your garden, and you let your friends know, and I promise you will begin to receive plants, bushes, wind chimes . . . all kinds of things for your beautiful garden!

- **Make a sign or have a plaque or a stone made to designate this as your special garden.** I had a large beautiful stone etched with "Garrett's Garden."

- **If you don't have the space for planting a garden, set aside a place on your deck or your porch to grow potted roses.**

- **Water features offer sounds of peace flowing.** Even the smallest fountain makes a peaceful sound.

- **Care for your plants, nurture them, prune them, watch them sprout, bloom, change, and wither, only to come back again in the spring.**

- **If you don't want to plant, give yourself a gift of buying flowers** at the grocery store or flower stand. They will brighten your home and your spirit. Remember, flowers awaken and soothe your spirit with their gifts of color, scent, and glorious beauty.

THE CREATIVE SPIRIT
IS A HEALING SPIRIT

It is often said that the mind becomes more creative when in chaos.

Funny thing about tragedy, it often makes the mind more active and when the mind is awake, it recalls memories, heightens imagination, and lets you view life through different eyes.

You will never be closer to God than you are right now. You are in a wounded state, having lost your beautiful child, but you are growing a new place in your heart to hold your child.

It's the arms of acceptance, and God is holding you and helping you see that.

> *"The Lord is close to the brokenhearted and*
> *saves those who are crushed in spirit."*
> **-The Bible**, Psalms 34:18 (NIV)

Your mind is awakening to creating a world where you must feel and embrace your child in other ways. It cries out to restore peace and harmony.

The Zen Buddhist Monk, Thich Nhat Hanh, says death is like a cloud in the sky. When it disappears, it doesn't mean the cloud has died. The cloud continues in another form like rain or snow.

If you look up to the sky and the cloud is no longer there, the sky is just showing you a new way of looking at the cloud. Don't be sad, the cloud is now rain that waters your garden.

So now you must plant a garden and watch the flowers grow. When you see the flowers in full bloom, you gather them and make a bouquet for your kitchen table.

The next day you can photograph them or paint them. Frame your photograph or painting and hang it on your wall and know that every time you look at it, it will remind you of the beauty of your child in a new form.

Do you see how you are the creator of your future, now?

When my son died, my heart longed to find expression in new ways. I created my rose garden during my bereavement. It brought me a place of comfort and peace, and a monument to my child.

I also found creativity at the ceramics studio where I painted bowls, pitchers, and platters with roses. I often took my children to the studio, and they, too, came alive with artistic ability. Everyone received hand painted gifts that year.

Many people believe they're not creative, but everyone is. Just look back to your childhood. Did you ever build a sand castle at the beach? Did you finger paint on giant sheets of butcher paper?

Did you make buildings with Popsicle sticks? Did you mold animals with clay?

It doesn't matter how good you thought it was, or what others thought. Your memory of doing it may be jaded by teachers' grades or comments from others, but none of that matters.

Whatever you create now is perfect because God is compelling you to soothe the upheaval in your mind.

While the critical thinking of your left brain tells you that sadness is everywhere and can never be any different, your right brain, the creative side, is screaming that it needs to create peace and harmony in new ways.

Whether you express words in a journal, paint on a canvas, tend a garden, or create new recipes for your family, anything creative will help soothe the biochemistry in your brain.

In your creations you will recognize your child's spirit is represented in new forms. It can be beautiful photography, hand made pottery, paintings on canvas, collections of things you love, the desire to paint a room, or plant a vegetable garden.

In my son's death, I gave him life in the birth of his story. I chose to write about him in hopes that my story will help people like you get through the worst time in your life, the loss of your beautiful child.

Because I was compelled to use my creative spirit to write, I see now, my son's purpose on this earth was to help others through similar tragic losses. He could only do this by going to heaven.

For me, this is Garrett's resurrection to everlasting life.

Stepping Stones: Creative Activities
To Aid in Recovery

Art is a very powerful way in which to process memories and feelings about your child. Art gives you an opportunity to work with senses such as touch, sight, and sound as a way of connecting to the profound thoughts and feelings that words often can't express. Consider exploring some of the following arts as an outlet for your feelings and memories:

- **Go to a local ceramics studio where you can learn to work with clay or paint pieces that are already formed.** Working with your hands and painting allows you to explore shapes and colors. This process can be a calming opportunity for a meditative break.
- **Art Classes offer the gifts of putting your emotions on canvas in the form of color.** Choose an art class where you don't feel pressure to perform well. This is for you, and not to be graded or critiqued in any way.
- **Photography brings instant pleasure.** With the ease of digital cameras and cell phones today, there are so many options to create beautiful works of art. Look into programs like **iPhoto** and **Instagram** for many creative ways to publish and print.
- **Use magazines and old family photos to create remembrance collages that combine words, photos of your child, colors, shapes, and textures.** You will go

through a range of emotions as you put these feeling into art. **Frame Them!**

- **Go through all of your old photo files and create a special album of your child's life.** Take the time to pick a special album and arrange the photos in a timeline. Publish your album online to share with others.

Music is another outlet for creative expression. Music tunes the heartstrings and opens up sensory emotions to feeling life in a new way. Sing, if you like to sing. Dance if you like to dance. Play the piano, or learn a new instrument. You will be surprised how your brain is open to music because it soothes the soul.

- **Create Playlists of music in iTunes.** Music offers a way to instantly transform mood and can change your state of being. Create Playlists for different feelings. I have lists that make me happy, a list for my tears, a list for dancing, a list for reflecting, and a list to help me power up to face the day.
- **Consider learning to dance.** Not only will this fuel your creative soul, it will also be great exercise.
- **Join your choir or a singing group.** It's an opportunity to meet new people
- **If you play an instrument . . . wonderful** . . . if not and you've always wanted to . . . do it.

Hopefully you are keeping up with your journal, since it is a creative expression too. Perhaps you have the **gift of writing** and if so, consider this:

- **Start a blog** of your recovery, or a subject that inspires you. The easiest way to do this is to sign up on <u>www.Blogger.com</u> through Google.
- **Write poetry** of your feelings. Read the poem, **Be!** By James Dillet Freeman. (Look it up on the internet) His poetry is inspiring and helped me in my early months of grief. Then write your own thoughts in poetry.
- **Begin your book.** Now is the time to tell your story. Besides it being a great tool for your own healing, others will benefit from reading your grief journey. You can choose to publish it or not. This is for your recovery. You can choose to share, or not.

Many of you may find these exercises overwhelming, but I promise you, we are working on *actively* recovering joy in your life. You can choose to do nothing, or you can be the key to your own recovery by making the choice to be proactive. I promise you will not be controlled by sadness forever.

Find your creative gifts and you will find a valuable tool to redirect your sadness into peace, acceptance, and yes, even joy.

"Joy is the infallible sign of the presence of God."
-Pierre Teilhard de Chardin, French
Philosopher and Jesuit Priest

FIND A NEW WAY

Now is the time to thank your beautiful child for the time you shared together and the lessons you are learning from their loss.

There will come a time in your grief where you know it's the perfect time to compartmentalize the memories.

Six weeks after my son died, I wrote in my journal "Today I grieved deeply. I'm so afraid I will feel this way forever, but then I'm afraid not to feel it forever. I want to feel close with his life, not his death.

That day, I asked Melissa to come over to help me go through papers that Garrett's English teacher had given me. We took turns reading them out loud. I found myself studying his homework, as I would have, had he been alive.

I was correcting his grammatical errors, looking for proper structure, and most of all, feeling so proud of the incredible gift he had of expressing himself. He always wanted to be a writer, like his mom and dad, and within those papers was proof he had done it. His English teacher had marked all of them *"A."*

Look for those little signs of completion and accomplishment in your child's life and treasure them. Even if your child was an infant, put his baby blanket on display. If he died before birth, frame his ultrasound photo. If he was a toddler, celebrate his first step by putting his baby shoes in a glass box. If he was in kindergarten, frame his first finger painting. If he was an accomplished baseball player, put his cap in a shadow box. These are proof to *you* that your child had a life to be acknowledged and it's the sum total of all the little milestones that will give you some peace in knowing they had a circle of life.

I kept Garrett's room exactly the same for almost six months. His bed unmade, his backpack on the floor where he left it, his toothbrush on his bathroom counter.

One day, I woke up and knew I didn't have to keep it that way any longer. I realized the enshrinement of his room and things left a dark pall on our home. It was as though we tiptoed around the fact that Garrett's things were still there, but why?

As I continued my healing path, I realized the need to have his room exactly the same was no longer necessary and it was damaging to my living children and husband. It made them feel as though Mommy will be sad forever because Garrett was never coming back.

Include your children in decisions about what to do with their sibling's belongings. As you work through your own processes of grief and remembrance it's critical to consider how each of your surviving children wishes to remember their lost sibling.

It's important to let your children help you with the process. It will give them a sense of helping you and will also help them put their feelings and memories in a good place.

After the children claimed the things they wanted, I called Garner and Sheila Simmons, good friends since before Garrett was even born. They arrived with stacks of giant rubber bins.

"We agreed to keep everything," I said, "just store it. One step at a time . . . right?"

That was the most I could handle at that point. Over the years, I've gone through the boxes and gifted things to people when the time was right, meaning . . . when I no longer felt the need to hang on to every physical thing connected to him. I also realized that others would really treasure some of his things.

I, of course, saved the things that meant the most to me; like, his baby shoes, his superman cape, his football, his letterman jacket, pictures, and everything he ever wrote. Those particular things are still with me, and his love remains everywhere, just a thought away.

Stepping Stones: Memory Books and Boxes

One of the most heart-wrenching and painful steps in grieving the loss of your child is the process of organizing, gifting, and packing his or her personal items, toys, and clothes. Take this process in steps so you can slowly gift or donate items as you proceed with your recovery.

Discuss a timeline and plan with family members. Include your partner, the child's siblings, or loved ones who may want to be involved in the process.

- **Look at your list of friends and decide who to ask for help with practical aspects of this process** such as getting packing materials or contacting organizations regarding donations.

- **Spend some time in your child's room connecting to your feelings and memories** and allow other family members to do the same.

- **Encourage family discussions about your child's personal items** and what you'd all like to do with them.

- **Look for those significant things that defined your child's life.** Even if your child was an infant, put his baby blanket on display. If he was a toddler, celebrate his first step by putting his baby shoes in a glass box. If he was in kindergarten, frame his first finger painting. If he was an accomplished baseball player, put his cap in a shadow box. These are proof to *you* that your child had a life to be acknowledged and it's the sum total of all the little milestones that will give you some peace in knowing they had a circle of life.

- **Decide what you'd like to frame.** I took Garrett's bulletin board to the art store and had them frame the whole thing, just as it was. It represented who he was at the moment he died. It was filled with things like hockey tickets, song lyrics, silly pictures, photographs, lists of things to do, people's phone numbers, and the number for the local pizza shop. It was a composite of him.

- **Create boxes of specific items.** These can be sports equipment, clothes, books, toys, or schoolwork. Some of these you may wish to keep and give to others over time when the opportunity presents itself. Taking time to gradually gift items allows you to move fluidly though the grief process as opposed to clearing out items at one specific time.

- **When you are ready to let some things go, consider donating** items to organizations that hold a special memorial meaning or offer items to close friends of your child's.

- **Consider a public memorial in honor of your child.** Plant a tree in your local park, build a bench at your child's school, or donate a special set of books to your library. Ask your friends and family for suggestions.

- **In your journal/workbook write down where you are storing certain things.** Trust me, you will forget, and then you'll go out of your mind trying to find it.

Stepping Stones: Anniversaries, Holidays, and Birthdays

Even in the best of times, holidays, birthdays, and anniversaries can be stressful. When you've lost a child, the absence is a giant hole on those significant days.

Be prepared for your feelings. Sometimes, I found the anticipation of the anniversary harder than the actual day. Consider arming yourself with a plan.

- **Plan, plan, plan.** The birthday or anniversary of the death of your child is a significant milestone in your grieving process. Don't leave it up to chance. By planning, you will actively take charge of the day. If you decide it's a day you want to spend feeling sad, so be it. Invite a friend to do it with you.

- **Create New Rituals** that include memories of your child. Otherwise, the loss will be like the elephant in a room.

- **Ask your living children, or your child's friends to help you with ideas** for honoring your child on these monumental days.

- **On the anniversary of the birth or the death of your child, make plans** with your spouse, family, or friends to do something. Don't leave the day to chance. It's too easy to fall into depression. Make plans, and you will have something to look forward to.

CONNECTING . . .
REACHING OUT ON
THE INTERNET

"The world needs the sense that we are all in it together."
-Jean Houston, interviewed on Oprah's Super
Soul Sunday and author, **The Wizard of Us**

Sometimes we find comfort from people and places we least expect. This chapter could not have been written when my son died. Nothing like it existed.

Social Media has changed the way people seek connection with others, and the way people grieve. It also offers a powerful tool in seeking massive, life changing prayer. It's a whole new level of connection in our society.

Through social media, we have the ability to celebrate lives *and* share our pain. The strength of it comes when you reach out and you are suddenly surrounded by massive numbers of people willing to offer a kind word, a story, an uplifting photo, or a life-changing prayer.

It can also be an opportunity to share your child's beautiful life in photos, words, and videos. It's one more way to communicate and check in with your family and friends.

You may question why you would share personal information, but the response to reaching out can bring you comfort in ways you've never dreamed. It also makes *others* feel good. You are offering them a way to make a difference in your life.

I guarantee you will have an opportunity to return the kindness. You see, no one is without pain or suffering in some way. It's also true that we all experience loss at some time in our lives. Great empathy surrounds us, as parents who have lost children, because losing a child is a tragedy that others can hardly even fathom. Just imagining your depth of despair breaks their hearts. That's why it's called *"the worst that could happen."*

Using social media recalls the fundamental traditions in grieving, lost in our society in the last few decades. Many years ago, people gathered as a community after a loss. It changed when families were no longer located in one community for a lifetime. We spread across the globe as our lives became filled with job transfers and obligations, separating us from old friends and family.

Enter social media, and our lives changed forever. It created a smaller world and a bigger community. We reconnected with childhood friends and distant cousins.

Social media enables an easier way to search for those who are like-minded and those we had connections with 20 years ago

We also are able to find people who have been through difficult times. And perhaps . . . connect with someone else who has experienced *the worst that could happen.*

It's a place to vent, feel sadness, share recovery, and draw from others who have walked before you. It can offer inspiration even in the middle of a sleepless night. Someone is always up with you in the darkness.

You can post "I'm really missing my beautiful child" and you will get immediate response from people saying they are praying for you, or a smile, or a hug. There is power in a sense of community.

Why do people care? It's human nature to have empathy and want to help those that are struggling. Social media makes the call for help *urgent*.

Doubters may say otherwise but it has been my experience that people want to surround you with love and compassion. The depth of connection might surprise you as you reach out.

There are numerous "chat rooms" for parents like us. What is a chat room? It's a website where online conversations are held in real time by a number of users who are typically like minded or share a specific interest or experience.

I chose Facebook as my main social network. I'm careful whom I choose as friends, and I make use of privacy settings.

My greatest joy is when I get unexpected posts from Garrett's friends who share a special memory or story with me from long ago. It's like receiving post cards from heaven. Sometimes they will post pictures I have never seen. There was even a video of my son at camp. His friends still find me after all these years . . . and they still care. What a gift.

Just as people will offer you their warmth and kindness, it's important you acknowledge others in the same way. Being sensitive to other's need for prayer and support will help you heal your own heart. We are meant to be on this planet together, interacting in a loving way. It's give and take. It's humanity.

If you have no idea how to use social media, I suggest you take a class or ask a teenager. Just be certain you choose the right friends to communicate with online and never post personal information that could put you in jeopardy in any way (for example, never post that you are going on a trip).

Social media should by no means replace therapy or the need for support groups. Some support groups offer Private Facebook Pages where you can have a forum for discussion with a select private group.

This is a relatively new way to work on grief recovery. It's not a perfect fit for everyone, but worth a try.

I will never forget the day my son's high school girlfriend found me 17 years later on Facebook. It still brings a smile to my face and joy in my heart. Now, we share memories, but more importantly, we are sharing the joyful "present" and all the present moment has to offer.

Stepping Stones: Seeking Comfort in Unexpected Places

You say, "'I didn't grow up with this, I can't do it!' But you didn't grow up driving a car and you learned."—**Gary Vaynerchuk**, *social media expert, author,* **Crush It**

The Internet and Social Media could possibly be a good resource of comfort for you.

- **Consider signing up for Facebook** and create an intimate group of friends you know. The conversations are more intimate in that you are not limited to the length of your post. With Twitter you are only allowed 160 characters.
- **Use privacy settings and caution in forming alliances with people online.** Only "friend" people you know or are referred to you.
- **To find a group, do a web search or a search on Facebook.** Somewhere you will find a comfortable place to share your thoughts. Your therapist can also recommend a group.
- **Research "chat rooms" for parents who have lost children.** I found one that was monitored by Melody Beattie, the author of **The Grief Club.** She lost a child and her website offers chat rooms for loss. (See resources at www.SandyPeckinpah.com)
- **Ask your therapist or bereavement group director** for their recommendations on online help.

- **Google Search is your greatest resource** for finding tools on the web.
- **Pinterest** and Instagram are beautiful ways to share pictures of your child. It's a photo-based social media.
- **If you don't understand how it works and wish to implement social media** in your recovery, consider taking a class at your community center, or contact a friend who can guide you.

PATTERN INTERRUPTERS AND RECOVERING INTIMACY

"People have a hard time letting go of their suffering. Out of a fear of the unknown, they prefer suffering that is familiar."
—**Thich Nhat Hanh**, Zen Buddhist Monk, teacher, author

Do you ever experience moments in time when you're sure people have been put there as angel messengers? By their presence, something changes in you.

It was in our year of grief. David was executive producer on a CBS/USA show, "Silk Stalkings." David buried himself in work after our son died. Working on the show was a displacement of grief for brief periods of time. There, he could transport himself into the world of television magic and forget his tragic loss.

When he came home at night, however, the reality returned and we struggled to find balance in our relationship that had been hit off balance by grief.

David's co-executive producer, Stu Segall and his wife Wendy offered us a break in the deepest hours of our sorrow with a gift of grace. They gave us tickets and accommodations for a trip to Italy. It was gift of light in the midst of darkness.

I loved Italy since I was sixteen and spent several months there traveling with a show called Up With People. David loved my stories of Italy, and we both loved the culture and the food.

As we've discussed in previous chapters, the loss of a child can suck the life out of a marriage. It had been 3 months since Garrett died, and David and I struggled with intimacy. We'd still give each other a quick kiss at the beginning and end of the day, but anything more seemed unbearable. Touching would give rise to emotion and transitioned quickly into sadness.

I remember clearly, David and I slept better on the plane than we had in the months. It was like being in a safe little cocoon, slumbering to the sound of jet engines.

We took a taxi from the airport into Rome and arrived at the Hassler Hotel located at the top of the Spanish Steps.

Exhausted, we followed the bellman to the second floor. He opened the door and gestured for us to enter. The room was decorated in bright sunny yellow, every bit of it. Yellow wallpaper, yellow bedding, and yellow drapes. It was impossible not to smile. It was an odd feeling to feel spontaneous joy.

We unpacked, and then ventured out in search of our first cappuccino. As we wandered the cobblestone streets, I could see David begin to relax, and so did I.

We entered a coffee bar and David ordered "due cappuccini" (two cappuccinos). He paid with lire (Italian currency before Euros) and used the word "grazie" over and over. He had no idea how much he gave the "barista," but the man seemed satisfied . . . until . . . we sat down at the table. The barista began shouting at us!

David quickly pulled out money from his pocket and placed it on the bar. The man nodded, grabbed the money, and turned away.

We left the bar and laughed hysterically until we couldn't laugh anymore. We learned later, cappuccinos are one price standing at the bar, and another sitting at a table. It was a monumental moment, however . . . it was laughter that broke through grief and freed us from pain.

That experience was enough uncertainty, though, for David. As soon as we returned to the hotel, David asked the concierge to hire a guide for the entire week.

"Angelo" arrived the next morning in a dark blue suit, Feragamo loafers, starched shirt with cuffs, and a perfectly knotted tie. We embarked on the "private tour" of Rome in his 1985 Mercedes. I mean the *really* private tour.

Our first stop, the Vatican. Angelo whisked us past the long line. We entered St. Peter's Basilica through giant doors and I felt a wave of sense memory since I'd been in the Vatican when I was sixteen. I looked to the right and there stood the Pieta, in the place I remembered; only now it was enclosed in protective glass.

It's a masterpiece of Renaissance Sculpture created in 1498-1499 by Michelangelo. It portrays the lifeless body of Jesus sprawled across the lap of his mother, Mary. When I first viewed it in 1968, I remembered feeling emotional, even tears.

I looked at the sculpture through present eyes and I now understood. Mary was a mother who lost her beautiful boy, and that part of her, I now shared

I couldn't possibly have known then, what it was like to *have* a child, nor how it felt to *lose* a child. Perhaps my soul knew that such a loss was my destiny.

Angelo led us through the Basilica and into the Sistine Chapel. It was in the process of restoration and closed to the general public, but somehow Angelo got us in. We stood in reverential awe.

Angelo broke our silence, "Okay, David, Sandy, You see-ah something now-ah" he waved his finger back and forth like a teacher, and continued, "no one else-ah see-ah."

He pulled a large key from his pocket and guided us to a door just outside the chapel. As we entered there were a dozen or so artists. They were restoring great works of art that would once again hang in the Vatican.

Angelo then led us upstairs to the Pope's sitting room. He had keys to mysterious doors that opened private places. We viewed the display of garments from past Popes, and looked out the second story window to view St. Peter's Square.

We toured the gardens in full spring bloom. Men in robes sat quietly on benches dozing in the late morning sun.

The past few months after Garrett's death, I had been numb to everything but the pain. I looked, now at the beautiful gardens of the Vatican and felt my spirit awaken to beauty and awe again. I felt like Garrett was with me, but not in sorrow.

Returning to our hotel at night, David and I set out to wander the streets of Rome. The scented nights were intoxicating and we delighted in exploring piazzas, fountains and statues. On those enchanted evenings, we re-captured our sense of "happy."

David kissed me in front of the Trevi Fountain, and we found our physical love rise up and renew itself.

On our last full day in Italy, Angelo drove us outside of Rome on winding roads into the countryside, entering a magical, tree-shrouded kingdom deep in the woods.

We pulled up to an old brick building. Part of it had worn away over hundreds of years and open to the sky. Tables were scattered around a huge wood-burning oven in the middle of the open-air restaurant.

Angelo quickly took command, seating me in view of the wood-burning oven to watch the chef direct "the show." The waiter brought menus and Angelo shook his finger "non, non." He ordered for us.

I had no idea I was about to enjoy one of the most euphoric meals of my life. It began with roasted red peppers and sliced fresh Mozzarella, drizzled with fragrant olive oil and aged Balsamic. Toasted Pine nuts dusted the top and fragrant basil was torn randomly over the plate. Crusty bread, warm from the oven was the final note in a symphony of flavors.

The next course came hot from the wood oven. It was a charred pillow of parchment paper, set onto a white platter. A present! The waiter broke open the paper. Inside was a perfect assemblage of handmade semolina linguini, fresh peas, cream, and pancetta; all scented with the heavenly aroma of smoked wood. The waiter brought aged Parmigiano cheese. I looked to Angelo and he nodded.

"Si, grazie," I replied.

I happen to love cooking, and I'm good at it. I've taken cooking classes throughout my life. I study Bon Appétit as though researching for a thesis. I appreciate creativity, the marriage of just the right ingredients, and exquisite presentation.

There are times in my life when all of those elements come together and I see, smell, and taste something that's so heavenly, it actually makes me cry. This was one of those moments. Angelo noticed my tears and put his hand gently on my shoulder and smiled. It was his grande finale.

To this day, I have no idea who Angelo was or how he ushered us into the secret places of Rome. Was it life changing? You bet.

It gave us the gift of reconnecting in our marriage and putting the grief from the tragic loss of our beautiful boy into a compartment we didn't have to access for a while. In fact, I don't remember ever crying once. Not once.

Except for the linguini.

"The greatest truth I have learned about happiness is that happiness is only ever one thought away at most." —**Robert Holden, Ph.D.** author, **Shift Happens!**

Stepping Stones: Pattern Interrupters, Reclaiming Joy

Grief can become a habit that's hard to break but this trip to Italy allowed us to break our pattern of heartache. I didn't feel I was betraying the loss of Garrett. Instead, David and I allowed ourselves to live again, just as our son would have wanted.

"Pattern Interrupters." are ways to *interrupt* the emotion of sadness, depression, or grief that can become routine after a tragedy or challenge in life. You must never let sadness control your life.

- **Interrupt your "Pattern of Sadness," or "Pattern of Anger," or any pattern that is holding your life hostage by making a plan to do something out of the ordinary.** It doesn't have to be as huge as a trip to Europe. It can be a hike in the mountains, a visit to the ocean, or a trip to visit a special friend.

- **If you decide to take a trip, ask someone from your Lifeline to help you plan it, organize the itinerary, and pack for it.** I was panicked at the thought of having to make decisions and something as simple as packing was overwhelming. I asked my friend, Karen Baldwin, who was a former Miss Universe, to help me pack. She traveled for a year out of her suitcase. I knew she would be the expert. Not only did she show me packing tips, she also loaned me her luggage.

- **Sometimes going someplace with a friend instead of your partner can give you the break in sadness.** A few months after my son died, my BFF Melissa Gilbert, took me to a spa in San Diego. We spent 3 days with each other and enjoyed working out, eating healthy food, getting massages, and hiking the beautiful hills. I will never forget when we played water volleyball in the pool. I suddenly thought of nothing else but winning. As I slammed the ball over the net with my fist, it smashed Melissa right in the face. For a second I was horrified, but then she started to laugh. I almost didn't recognize the sound of my own voice as it rose up from an unfamiliar place inside of me, and then both of us laughed uncontrollably. In fact, we were admonished for being too noisy by the massage room monitor nearby. We still couldn't stop laughing!

- **Don't let the loss of your child ruin the quality of your life every day.** It's very hard to do, but only *you* can break the pattern. Each day, Allow yourself time to feel sad, but then recognize the joys you still have. It can be hard when you've experienced such a tragic loss. That's when interrupting a pattern of emotion is most important.

- **Take time for your spiritual well being.** Read inspiring books to help you interrupt your habit of grief. Visit online inspirational sites.

- **Tears of sadness and tears of Joy have a different chemical make-up.** Set aside the time for crying, but then turn those tears into tears of joy for the good memories that reside in your brain and your heart.

- **It's important to try to find a reason for laughing every day.** Watch your cat chase a piece of yarn, or find laughter in renting a great comedy for a movie night with your family. Animal videos on **www.YouTube.com** **always** make me laugh.

Above all, be open to the possibility there are miracles and people who deliver them. I am forever grateful for our trip to Italy. It was the first time I knew, after the deeply tragic death of my son, I could, in fact, experience intimacy with my husband and reclaim joy and laughter in my life.

Stepping Stones: Partner Relaxation and Sexual Connection

Coming together intimately and physically with your partner is a key part of the healing process. Sex may be the furthest from your mind, and you may even feel guilty or resistant about the idea of "indulging" in intimacy. Put any fears and discomforts aside and take time a few mornings or evenings a week to simply lie down with your partner in a quiet, private space.

- **Relaxing as a couple** is imperative to healing. It's purpose is to quiet the mind together and reconnect physically. Create a relaxing space with lighted candles and soothing music.

- **Close your eyes and relax your body.** You can find a comfortable position touching your partner's hand, chest, or body.
- **Breathe deeply and concentrate on feeling present and relaxed.** Allow yourself to deeply sigh.
- **If you're struggling to connect physically** you may simply want to practice repeated sessions of relaxation with simple touching, breathing, and a quiet space together before building to any further intimate or sexual sharing. It often leads to reconnecting sexually.
- **End your session by kissing your partner lovingly,** no matter what. This will conclude this exercise in a place of connection.
- **If you continue to struggle with reconnecting,** please don't hesitate to make an appointment with a therapist who specializes in sexual healing. It will save your marriage.

Understand that sexual connection will take some time and effort to reinstate in your relationship, but the reward is the closeness and intimacy ("into me you see" as Iyanla Vanzant says), that will keep your marriage healthy and alive.

AND LIFE GOES ON . . .

Breakthrough to Reclaiming Happiness and Joy

"The key will be to see all things in your life as GRACE. No matter what happens, if we are still, listen and see, we will find the Grace in it. Some of the biggest acts of Grace in my life have been unanswered prayers and seeming tragedy."
-Mastin Kipp, www.TheDailyLove.com

Once, I was a woman who believed in fairy tales. I believed if I was good, honorable and true, nothing bad could ever happen. What I realized is that no one is immune from tragedy.

I've come to understand that loss has two components that tie me to my son. One is the sadness that I couldn't hold him in my arms anymore. That's the emotional component. The deep, deep tears of emotional sadness, served a purpose in connecting him to me. It dissipates somewhat with time and healing. So much so, that now, down the road, I look back on it and miss the deep uncontrollable tears.

The other component is the physical connection I have inside every cell of my body that stays with me forever. Together, my husband and I merged our cells and created Garrett. He came from the miracle of "us." That cellular connection is a physical union of energy that never, ever dies.

With that connection I actually do have one more day . . . or many more days to hold my son, because he is inside of me, always.

What if I had just one more day to tell my son I loved him? No matter how many days you have with the one you lose, you will *always* wish you had one more day to say "I love you." Try to make peace with the fact you had just the right amount of days, and it was all God's plan.

When you're in the early weeks of grief, you don't think the pain will ever end. People say "Time heals all wounds," but it really doesn't. The death of your child is a wound that will leave a visible scar on your life forever, but it's a scar you can learn to live with. In fact, in the future, you will have days you don't even notice the scar at all.

There will come a time in your healing where you will simply be able to discipline your emotions and eject sadness from your life. You'll begin to notice days going by without a tear or a sigh. You'll hear yourself laugh and it will be an odd feeling, but feel so good.

Joy will begin to make brief appearances in your life, and you won't trust it at first. You will say, *How can I feel this way when my child died?"* But then it enfolds you in its peace and you'll welcome it like an old friend.

"Grief is not a diagnosis. It's a badge of honor."
-Robert Holden, author of **Shift Happens**

One sleepless night I was really missing my son. I was alone in my bed. I reached for my iPod on my bedside table. I scrolled through the Playlists looking for peace within music. I looked for music that could open my dialogue with God. I chose a meditation called "Awakenings."

As I closed my eyes, I sank into the vibration of trickling water and church bells. I drifted off to sleep, and found myself walking along a stretch of beach familiar to me. It was a block from my childhood home in California. As a teenager, I sought refuge there. I walked to the rocky shores nearly every day with my diary and pen in hand. I wrote volumes of teenage angst and drama. I also wrote dreams of my future while sitting amongst the rocks and the splashing waves.

In my dream, the sound of the foghorn announced the morning mist. It was a comforting sound. I climbed the rocks, and ocean waves sent sprays of salt air in my face. I suddenly wasn't a teenager anymore. I was as I am now, and I was wrapped in a tremendously heavy cloak and I knew it was called "Sadness." My chest was heavy and I struggled to breathe. There I was in my thoughts, back on that beach, alone.

And then, I wasn't alone. Sitting on the rock opposite me was God. I knew it was God because it was light, and *love* filled my being. I began to cry. Tears streamed down my face as He pulled me into Him and tilted my head to rest on His shoulder. I sank into him and I could breathe. The water washed around my feet.

I sobbed and dug my fingers into God, but he didn't push me away or even flinch.

I cried for every part of my life that felt loss. I felt perfectly safe unbridling my grief in this portal of peace, God's safe arms. There were no children needing me, or circumstances demanding my strength. With each crash of the waves I felt cleansed, and light flooded in, filling me with a sense of peace.

It was the moment I let my guard down and God came in to hold me up. I awoke wiping tears from my eyes, sat up in bed, and felt incredibly heavy in my body.

My God! What's wrong with me?

I jumped out of bed and walked in circles.

Did I die? Was my heart impossibly broken? I was just with God!

If I died, I didn't have to feel emotional pain anymore. But, *if* I died, my children would be alone and I am all they have.

I stood quietly holding myself up next to the bed when suddenly I felt like someone was pulling a long gossamer garment up from my feet over my legs, then hips, to my shoulders, and I felt my arms reach up as the ethereal fabric lifted overhead.

With every inch of the illusory cloak being stripped from my body, I felt the fear washing away. And then it was gone.

I had an incredible feeling of calm and I knew without a shadow of doubt what it was. The veil of sadness was lifted from my being. My heart was now forever healed, open, and free. I felt such incredible love, almost indescribable, and it was real.

I crawled back into bed and fell asleep. In the morning, I awoke knowing my life had transitioned. Was it a dream? I don't know. What I do know is that it was real enough to change my future.

I'd worked the steps of grief over the years and arrived at the other side, a soft gentle agreement with God that I had indeed found *acceptance* and opened a space in my heart for *joy*.

I began to pray and find stillness in every single day. I discovered hope for the chapters ahead. Grace was bestowed upon me.

The word Grace is defined by the Bible as the spirit of God that exists in humans for the soul's purpose of strengthening them.

I know I'm strong, I know I'm a better person, I know I'm a better mother because of losing my child. I never take a single day, even a single moment, for granted. I live in the present.

I know my faith became a permanent dwelling in my heart, and I no longer fear death. I know I can handle anything life brings my way. I know I am living a life of *resilience*.

Remember when I shared about walking the Red Carpet and believing I was living a fairy tale? Well . . . I discovered I actually *do* have a fairy tale life.

After all, what are fairy tales, but stories of triumph over adversity.

I have a joyful life today . . . and I never thought that would be possible after my beautiful boy died.

How do I know I'm healed? Because sadness no longer defines who I am. I realized I had the power within me to compartmentalize the grief of losing my son and could choose to feel the tears when I wanted to. It was like shedding the cocoon of sadness and a butterfly transformation to living a joyful life. I can still cry when I want to, but it doesn't feel out of control. Instead, there's a harmonious comfort to it as my heart connects with the sweet ballad of his memories.

I am able to look at the life of my son and marvel at the 16 years, 3 months, and 10 days I had with him. He was such a gift, and so were the lessons learned from his death.

For years now, I have guided many others through the grief process. It made my heart come alive with meaning and being of service!

My son's death opened a door before me . . . my purpose.

I suffered the greatest tragedy a mother could imagine, and I survived. Saying you're a survivor implies you have fought a war when in reality you rode the waves of life that the universe had planned for you all along. It's my story of triumph, and you will have one too.

I know for sure, God guided me to share my story so that you might resurrect your life from the shadows of sadness and find peace in the acceptance that your child died.

Yes, your child died and you will ultimately be at peace with that. You *will* reclaim joy and feel happiness again. You are on that path, now, and you will survive . . .

I promise.

RESOURCES

For up-to-date resources, please visit

www.SandyPeckinpah.com

For the newest blog, please visit

www.BreakthroughToHappy.com

In Gratitude

I am so grateful for the 16 years, 3 months, and 10 days I had with my beautiful boy, Garrett Denver Peckinpah.

I'm fortunate to have a family and a network of people in my life who care. Through the greatest joys and the deepest sorrows, they are there.

First and foremost, my faith kept me going, even when I thought faith was gone from my life, it hid in the crevasse of my heart that wouldn't stop beating.

Paula: Thank you for introducing me to David Peckinpah in Carmel, California so many, many years ago. Without that chance meeting, I would never have had the family and life I have. Your encouragement in writing this book surrounded me in a caring "blanket" of love and helped me through the process of finishing it. There's a reason why our friendship has withstood the test of time and spanned over 50 years. I love you, Amica.

David: I am so deeply grateful I was married to you, and together we created four amazing children. You were a wonderful husband and father. You left this earth to soon. I'm sure you died of a broken heart; the loss of our son was too much to bear. I will love you forever and look forward to seeing you and Garrett at the Pearly Gates.

Trevor, Julianne, and Jackson: Thank you for being the greatest gifts of my life. I am so very proud of each of you and treasure every single day of being your mother. You are the strongest children I know. You lost your brother and then your father, and yet you continue to smile and find meaning in life. Thank you for making me feel so loved. I will always be there for you, no matter what.

Melissa: Yet another triumph for our strand of pearls. When we met over 20 years ago, our bond was undeniable and continues to be after all these years with joys and sorrows, milestones, and transitions. Thank you for always being just a phone call away and never letting me cry alone. You gave me adventures and treasures that helped me find laughter again. We remain together in a way that can't be explained, it just is. Your greatest tribute brought me my greatest joy when you and Bruce named your beautiful boy, Michael Garrett Boxleitner. You honored my son in an everlasting way . . . remarkable. I am blessed to be his Godmother and watching him grow to be the amazing young man he is. How can I even express how much I love you? I can't, but our souls know . . . we will continue to be BFF's forever and ever, amen.

Marta: I couldn't have found my way back without you. I know that to be true. Thank you for being my therapist, guide, counselor, and keeper of my family's well being.

Nan: My wonderful friend. It seems as though your beautiful voice is the soundtrack of our history together. It documents all of our milestones beginning with Up With People. Thank you for your wisdom, your expertise, and your guidance with this book. As we both know, you've seen it all . . . my tears, my soul, and my heart through many lifetimes.

Peter: Thank you for loving us so much. You are the music and the heartstrings of our past, present, and future.

My Family: I have the best family in the world. Mom and Dad, brothers and sisters, nieces and nephews . . . the certainty of a strong family carries you forward in life no matter what happens. I'm grateful we treasure our family Thanksgivings together. It gave me something to look forward to every year. The bond it's creating for our children is priceless.

Jody: I treasure the times we had together when our children were small. Thank you for giving me the inspiration of a garden. It helped me heal and taught me that nature always has a plan.

Karen: You always knew the right thing to say, the right thing to do, and held my hand as we made some of the toughest decisions of my life. The hours we spent together writing, crying, laughing . . . I know it's what helped me through it all. I am so grateful when you remind me of the sweet memories and the moments I've forgotten. You never forget and that is your greatest gift to me.

Jack: Thank you for sleeping on our couch, holding us by the hand when we had to make difficult choices, caring for us, and being Godfather to my beautiful son, Jackson.

Rosa: You mean the world to me. Thank you for taking care of our home and our hearts. You always treated my children like your own. I love you and your wonderful family.

Trisha: To this day, our friendship has endured, our lives intertwined, and I have the privilege of watching your children grow. Thank you for being Garrett's first babysitter and staying a part of our lives forever. I love that you still find the time to lay flowers on Garrett's grave. You and Milos have honored him so greatly in giving your son his name.

Gidget: My forever friend. Your home and heart were always a safe haven for me, and my children. I don't think you even realize what a big heart you have. Thank you for, once again, providing the most glorious day of my life . . . my wedding and the acknowledgement that "I've survived!"

The Packer Family: When I think of Garrett's childhood, I think of you with such delight. What a wonderful time that was on Cerrillos Drive. Georgie, you will forever remain Garrett's first best friend.

Gar and Sheila: Thank you for your friendship, your guidance, your encouragement, and your love for our family. Thank you for being the keeper of our family history, the truth and the myths. Both shaped the Peckinpah Family. We will always remain connected.

Randi: I'm so grateful you encouraged me to stay committed to working out. I know our mornings together helped release the endorphins to help me heal. Our friendship has sure seen it all, and somehow we've exercised *through* it all!

Kim, thank you for being my friend and helping me resurrect a new life in a new town. You listened tirelessly to my stories and make "our job" so much fun.

My girlfriends: Those I've mentioned, and those I've kept private. You are my circle of love and protection. You all know how much you've meant to me, and how you've carried me through. I will always be there for you, just as you have for me.

Walter: Thank you for being a muse and encouraging me to never stop writing, even when there were times I expressed to you, that my story was too painful to put into words. You said "keep going, this is important." Writing changed the pain into purpose.

Amy B: Thank you for helping me develop the exercises for this book. Your help was my launching pad.

Emily: You were Garrett's first and only love. The night before he died, he was planning his Christmas gift for you. Thank you for reconnecting with me. Your connection brings me such happiness.

James Lawrence de Girolamo: You've captured my heart, my soul, and my spirit. Falling in love with you gave me a safe place to hold my heart. You honor my past and allow me to express my sorrow. I put my head on your shoulder and find peace. You celebrate my living children, you honor my beautiful boy Garrett, *and* you acknowledge and honor the man that brought these beautiful children into this world with me. I've found my joy and bliss with you. I'm happier than I ever could have imagined and I look forward to every day with you.

I've had a lifetime of lessons to learn the truth.

Life has taught me that things don't always happen the way we think they should.

I've learned that love never dies. It's the most important human experience there is. It's a privilege and a commitment and not always easy. I've learned that being a mother is a gift and every single day is a gift with your child. I've learned that friends and family want to help if you allow it. And . . . I've learned there is something called "resilience" that, when activated, allows us the joy of living again.

After losing Garrett, and then David, I thought my heart would never heal.

But it did.

ABOUT THE AUTHOR

Sandy Peckinpah is on a mission to help heal your past, transform your future, and "breakthrough to happy."

She discovered the power in storytelling when she was inspired to write her first book, <u>Rosey . . . the Imperfect Angel</u> after the birth of her daughter. Julianne was born with a severe facial defect, a bilateral cleft lip and gum. It would take numerous surgeries to repair her face and through the process Sandy and her family learned the beauty of imperfection.

The fairy tale caught the attention of news media throughout the country. Sandy and her daughter appeared on national television talk shows (including **ABC, NBC** and **Fox**), radio programs, and in newspaper articles and magazines throughout the U.S. It helped raise awareness about children born with this disfiguring, but repairable, birth defect.

Rosey . . . the Imperfect Angel was recorded as a CD, produced by Tony Award Winner, **Michael Alden**, who also wrote the music, recorded by the **Moscow Symphony Orchestra**. It starred the voice of actress and former SAG President, **Melissa Gilbert**, best known for her portrayal as Laura Ingalls in **Little**

House on the Prairie. The CD made it all the way to the **Grammy Ballot** in 2009!

Her second book, **Chester the Imperfect All Star**, followed with the same media attention. Her fairy tales continue to bring enlightenment, wonderment, and hope to children and are used in schools, hospitals, and clinics to raise awareness and help children with self-esteem.

Story telling and fairy tales were a predominate theme in Sandy's life. She worked closely with her late husband, David Peckinpah, who was the executive producer and writer of numerous television series including the Emmy nominated CBS series **Beauty and the Beast,** Sci-Fi's **Sliders,** and USA Network's **Silk Stalkings**, along with numerous television movies and the Disney box office hit, **Man of the House**. Sandy ran the operation of their film company, including developing ideas, storylines, and editing scripts, and also worked as an actress in television movies and series.

She collaborated with life-long friend, noted San Francisco interior designer **Paula McChesney to** write **Passion by Design,** a blueprint for designing and living a life of passion. With Paula, she co-hosts the radio show, **Passion By Design**, on AM Talk Radio in California (Past shows can be downloaded on **iTunes**).

Sandy tragically lost her oldest son at the age of 16 from Spinal Meningitis. Her book **How to Survive the Worst that Could Happen** was inspired by her own intimate story, woven with her research and experience to offer a book that shifts the odyssey of grief from one of passive submission into a faster, active recovery. In the process, she learned how to help others rise up from life's most challenging and difficult transitions.

Sandy enjoys working with people who are serious about transforming their future. She has enlightened and guided others to discover how the hidden magic of their own unique story, no matter how tragic, can awaken the future of possibility and be their **"Breakthrough to Happy."**

Sandy enjoys life with her husband, Jim de Girolamo, and her beautiful children in sunny Southern California.

To read more stories, visit her blog: www.BreakthroughToHappy. com. She welcomes your comments!

If you'd like Sandy to speak to your organization, be a guest on your show, or inquire about products and services, please contact her on her website: **www.SandyPeckinpah.com**.

CPSIA information can be obtained at www.ICGtesting.com
Printed in the USA
LVOW08s0242030414

380130LV00001B/47/P